The Dangerous Sort

When George's Grandmamma was told
That George had been as good as Gold
She promised in the Afternoon
To buy him an *Immense* BALLOON.
  And
      so she did; but when it came,
It got into the candle flame,
And being of a dangerous sort
Exploded
      with a loud report!

From *Cautionary Tales for Children* by H. Belloc
(Gerald Duckworth and Co. Ltd.)

The Dangerous Sort

The Story of a Balloon
by
ANTHONY SMITH

Photographs selected and arranged
by
Douglas Botting

London
GEORGE ALLEN AND UNWIN LTD

© George Allen & Unwin Ltd., 1970

ISBN 0 04 629014 1

PRINTED IN GREAT BRITAIN
in 12 point Plantin type
BY JOLLY AND BARBER LIMITED, RUGBY

CONTENTS

CHAPTER 1

Survivors' Dinner

A balloon cannot be anything but beautiful. The shape has a purpose and a delicacy to it which is acutely correct. Like a waterfall it is always majestic, and size or kind are irrelevant. Like a girl holding a lighted candle, or a boat slicing through the water, there are various features of life whose beauty is eternal. It just so happens that a balloon is one of them.

To fly by balloon is to experience a great privilege. 'Each time, I am reborn', says a Swiss. Nothing is quite the same again. It is a destiny without a destination. It is pointlessness which gives great purpose. It is enchanting. It is funny. It is idiotic. It is supreme. It cannot last and yet endures. There is a greatness about it which then becomes cowpats and wet grass at the landing. There is a transformation, a leap from earth, a long leap, a glorious improbable leap, and then a tangle of ropework and laughter and unrelenting earth. There is also fear, and sudden unwelcome sounds can be most loud in that silent world a mile above the land. The ropes are inaudible on earth; up there they talk with authority. The balloon's fabric is a lowly stuff until it is filled and buoyant; and then it is recreated into something to transport you, to pick you up and put you down, to let you live with fervour, to let you die with ease.

It is weird, and right, and yet out of context to be up there. There can be an arrogance which ought to be quelled, as it asserts that all lower things are lesser things. Too much ebullience is intolerable and it is fortunate that circumstance can always put a stop to it; the greater the previous pomp the greater the subsequent collapse. Take the case of the cascading slate.

It had been a glorious summer's day. All around and beneath us had been the soft enchantment of the English countryside. We had seen deer plunging over the tussocks, and hares and rabbits on every side. We had seen the delicate tracery of interwoven patterns as tractor wheels had gone this way and that, as combine harvesters

had eaten up the corn concentrically, and as the feet of sheep had trodden paths on flat fields, on steeply contoured hills. We had seen the earth, and we had seen that it was good.

That was our undoing. It filled the five of us with an effervescent joy. We burbled and shouted as our cups ran over. We called everyone. We yelled from the tree-tops, and we made even louder noise when the distance was greater, when we had either risen further into the atmosphere or they had been left behind. I think we were intolerable, but wholly without malice and merely incapable of a decent restraint. As it was, we remorselessly poured out our excessive libations upon the all and sundry of that piece of rural England.

A village appeared dead ahead. It lay in a slight hollow as it had done since its medieval beginnings. It had a church and a line of chestnuts, and much thatch and many people, and we decided to make a low descent over its utter tranquillity. Fortunately we were already losing height at the time and the plan was to check this descent with a suitable dusting of sand over the very centre of the village. Not only would we then ascend comfortably without landing on some house-top but we would have poured further disdain upon their heads.

The smooth descent was excellent. At some ten miles an hour we both travelled towards that village and dropped deeper into it. From 200 feet above we became 100 feet above, and the objective grew nearer and larger. The trees and houses followed the slope of the hill, and we too ran down that slope with similar ease. It soon seemed as if all the villagers had been collected into the main street, for that was so packed and the rest was so empty. A procession perhaps; a fête; some jamboree, totally English in its improbable ritual. The thoughts

welling by motor
cle from Capetown
Cairo would jerk
one's thoughts in
our of gentler forms
ransport. Jules
ne's fictional balloon
age across Africa
vided an excellent
cedent.

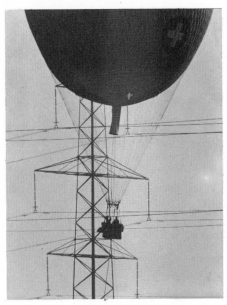

Unfortunately, modern living and the ancient sport of free ballooning proved not to be in total harmony. The old days had gone for good.

added fresh and quite unnecessary fuel to our own junketings. We called at them yet harder, but they did not call back. We may even have called them names, but I cannot remember because a suspicion was swelling rapidly that this was no ordinary jamboree.

It was solemn. It was indeed a procession, and led towards the church whose square squat tower stood straight ahead. We were instantly silenced by a realization and then by the sight, as a further tree passed beneath us, of fresh soil around a dark hole. With the stopping of our talk there was suddenly a lessening of the wind, or seemingly so for we appeared to hover above that ceremony as the first of the mourners passed through the brown wooden gate. The coffin was there too, but above those pall-bearers with their small and heavy load were we, utterly quiet and monstrously obtrusive. Above those small garlands of flowers, tied with string to the box's handles, was our basket tied with its own ropework to the huge, globular, orange shape above. We were enormous, partnered only by our equally enormous shadow, and we pretended not to be there. They too, for their part, gave no sign of having detected our existence, and a couple of hundred pairs of eyes were cast down in the hope that the monstrous orange thing would go away.

The wind then dropped almost to nothing, as if equally stilled by the solemnity. All the people were quiet, and even the jackdaws settled back on the trees. We too were as silent as that yawning hole, and were moving at a correctly funereal pace. Unfortunately, and this fact became plainer and plainer, our descent was still continuing. Without one doubt we would soon hit something, certainly the church and probably its tower, unless we took action. Ready in my hands was the only libation to avert such inevitability; but it remained there. How could I, so largely instrumental in invading their privacy,

Everything had undoubtedly been easier in those old days, whether setting off on a Gordon Bennett race from Brussels (above) or for an afternoon's pleasure from Hurlingham (below).

pour further scorn by showering their ceremony with sand? It would be no mere handfuls at this late stage in the emergency, but sackfuls at 30 lbs of ballast a time. The invasion was bad enough. To add bombing to the insult was yet greater treachery. So the first sack remained poised, unthrown and unpoured, and we coasted gently along 80 feet above their still unsandy heads.

Such restraint, however commendable, made the forthcoming impact yet more certain. The point of collision narrowed itself down from the church in general to the tower in particular, and to the left-hand side of that tower. Although we had not cast sand upon the mourners it would surely destroy our slightly enhanced image if we were to follow such thoughtfulness by wrapping ourselves around the tower, liberating our hydrogen into it and then igniting (for such is the custom of this type of accident) the entire structure. All earlier consideration and restraint would surely be forgotten in the general disruption, quite apart from an additional need for further holes in the ground.

The tower loomed. The mourners mourned. The disaster approached most effortlessly. There was nothing now to be done, save to pour two sackfuls of sand on to the slated roof beneath us. The noise was unforgettable. The jackdaws leapt into the air. The procession had to look up. Dislodged slates rattled slowly down that steep-sided roof, and kept up their own clatter for an age before falling to the ground, one by one.

'Sorry', I said, 'terribly sorry.'

And with that we went our way, fortunately missing the tower.

The village dropped away beneath us, and the long file of silent faces became circles of shapes draped around that grave. Our retreat was absolute. From vastness we became a speck. There may have been the silence of death down below, but it was as nothing compared with the chastened hush within our basket. The five of us looked outwards, either at the eternity of sky or the patchwork intricacies of the land now, so comfortingly, some 3,000 feet beneath our feet.

The peculiarity of this form of aviation is largely a matter of entirely contrary events, either happening one after the other or simultaneously. Idiocy, danger, beauty, grace and ungainliness, enchantment and despair – they all enter the lists. Once, at an ascent from Eindhoven, some clown was so infected with the general gaiety of a balloon's take-off that he gave a great unobserved push to the basket as it climbed from his reach. As pilot I relaxed because the rate of ascent seemed more than adequate. Moments later, when that man's thrust had lost its impetus, we were plummeting straight towards the hooting, speeding, swerving nightmare of an arterial road. Another occasion, when 18,000 feet up somewhere near St Moritz, and when drinking deep of the Alpine world on every side, a supersonic jet flashed by. We never even saw it but the clap of noise thundered and thundered as it echoed around us, bouncing back and forth from all that angular landscape. Beauty and terror make intriguing bedfellows, sometimes complementing each other, sometimes succeeding each other to the exclusion of all else.

Jambo was the balloon in which I flew. Basically she was a thing of neoprene and cotton, of manilla net and ropes, of laminated wood, and her basket was of osier wickerwork through which ran eight

. where Douglas Botting,
dden balloon enthusiast,
s caring for otters.

stainless steel wires leading up to that wooden ring. Indeed she seemed no more than a confusion of all these physical things when coerced from downstairs cupboard to van, and then from van on to the grass of the take-off site. She became all these things again when, deflated and heavy, the whole lot had to be lifted, dragged and manoeuvred out of the landing field. Only between these two situations did the balloon Jambo assume her rightful character.

A person, they say, is a composite of elements fashioned into proteins, fats and the like, but certainly possessed of personality during a lifetime. A balloon, similarly fragmented, cannot be accused of such a personality when on the ground. Up in the air, when a danger has just been missed or when one's sense of wonder is brimming over, it is only too easy to forget reason, to credit the balloon with a kind of personal authority. Upon the final destruction of this balloon it was easier still to feel that something had gone beyond mere fabric, mere cord and ropes. Each experience with this most singular flying machine helped to heighten that stabbing sense of loss. On the day that Jambo exploded, many of us said, without a qualm and without hesitation, that something had died.

It had been born seven and a half years beforehand in and around

*sistance was sought
n every possible
rter, from Ralph
oth (top, left),
mer captain of the
oo, from Gerry Long
anding with him in
R.33), from
lin and Rosemary
udie (top centre) who
d flown and sailed
oss the Atlantic in
e Small World', from
arles Dollfus (bottom
) who is the world's
mier aeronaut, and
n Jo and Nini
sman (bottom centre)
Jacques Demenint
ht) who all run the
ly active Hague
loon Club.*

the Ganshoren district of Brussels. A couple of Belgian families had stitched and glued the fabric, fashioned the net, and spliced the rope. The result had been stuffed into green canvas sacks, flown to Africa, and examined for the first time in a hall substantially larger than a Belgian attic. In Zanzibar we inflated Jambo for the first time, and eventually took off for the mainland. On board we baptized the new balloon with champagne and, as we majestically flew over those Indian Ocean straits with uncanny simplicity, started to acquire a reverence for the thing of fabric and rope which was transporting us.

Subsequently everything seemed to happen in Africa. There were storms, unbelievable thermals and unforgettable sights, flights which became survival exercises and landings remarkable for the fact that no one was ever hurt. Those of us who flew in Jambo over the game parks, the escarpments and hot plains of Africa were increasingly amazed that the atmosphere could be so violent without the final outcome being disastrous. Like a ship driven helplessly towards rocks only to be tossed by some miraculous wave on to high ground, we walked away from each landing with a growing astonishment at our good fortune. Jambo, mere fabric, mere rope, was replaced in her canvas bags with greater and greater care and reverence.

That balloon safari idea had originated in my mind when bouncing from Cape Town to England on the back of a motor-bicycle. Surely, I had argued, the planet should be seen from above and without the raucous attendance of any engine. Later on, I was to long for the drifting balloon to have some form of motive power, however raucous. Anyhow, the African experiences had ended in March 1962 with a tale to tell, with excellent photographs, but with nerves considerably shaken by a steady witnessing of the narrow margin between survival and death. There must be some special agency acting for first-time fools, or so the three of us felt after that expedition. How else could we be flying back on a BUA freighter, entirely intact and with an un-damaged half-ton of balloon at our feet?

On board that plane, apart from the crew and us, and those canvas sacks, there were animals. As we placed food in the outstretched monkey hands, or clattered down the steps at Khartoum and Malta with as many leashed dogs as we could manage, for their relief, I felt a growing determination to see less of that narrow margin in the future. As we unwrapped leashes from bowsers and lorry wheels, I wondered what to do with the balloon. And as we tried to shut cage

Ballooning problems loomed larger when we first saw the number of 1-ton cylinders
necessary for one inflation. Everything in the lighter-than-air business suddenly
seemed infinitely heavier.

The completed sight of that first inflation added to our determination

doors on woolly, wiry, wriggling inmates, I thought the only rational course was to shut the balloon up in some cupboard, with affection but with firmness.

So much for reason. So much for rigid decision. 'Come to Europe with your balloon', said the Dutch couple who had taught me to fly. 'Let us see the thing we made', said the Belgians who had made it. 'Surely it is damaged beyond repair', said the sages who had predicted disaster. 'Let us have a flight', said the pilot who had taken me across to Holland at weekends for those training flights. 'Come to Dongen', said the organizers of a balloon gathering. 'Cable Please When Famous Jambo Plus Good Self Arriving Rotterdam', said the paper in my hand. And so it happened, with nothing more than a prayer from me for torrents or thunder or waterspouts or great wind in the area wherever the dreaded Dongen happened to be. Surely something would prevent the flight?

'It will not go into the car', I said as others were proving that it would. 'The basket on the roof will make us too high for the ferry', I said, shortly before some benign official singled us out for his especial care. 'We will be late', I said, and drove with absolute care and attention. 'We will never find the place.' Dongen, said the signpost, with pointed clarity. Ballonhaven, said some cardboard nailed to a tree. 'In that gate', said someone from the crowd. 'By No 6', said a man with Ballondienst on his arm. 'So you've arrived', said Jo, Nini, Jacques, Ben, Albert, François, Andrée, Jean, Wolfgang and Alfred. 'And where is Jambo?'

The very smell of the fabric was awesome, and all the handling and pulling and sorting evoked every African experience. However it was pleasant not being entirely alone. The European ballooning fraternity was there in strength with advice and balloons. They turned on their gas, and we turned on ours. We got into difficulties with a gust and insufficient sandbags. There were they wrestling with the same contrary wind. I had forgotten break-thread, and could immediately borrow some of theirs. Africa had been a solitary experience but Dongen was a community. Africa had sapped the courage from us and it was nice to feel a returning confidence.

I took off with a Dutch cameraman, a Dutch journalist and Geoffrey Hancock. Geoffrey, weekend pilot with the Tiger Club, had long since been promised a flight and acted as map-reader for the four of us. So I relaxed and felt the anxiety fall from my shoulders. Instead

We learned how to fly . . .
We learned how to land . . .

of the African turbulence there was gentle air and we sailed along at 1,000 feet with perfect equanimity. On every side were the other balloons, and their obvious stability added to our own. We even hailed each other when a shout seemed worth while, and we even understood each other when the distances were not too great. Admittedly the wind strengthened when we were up there, and the poplars flicked their tops obediently to its gustiness, but what was a wind when you were not alone? What was fear when the others were so obviously unafraid, as they tooted trumpets, cat-called, and floated equally in the sky?

A tinge of the old feeling returned as we approached for our landing. The wind was fast, and we could hear the trees. We saw our field, and we became quiet. We gently rushed at it. And then hit. It was a big hit, and an unaccountably high bounce. Why so high? Pull more on the valve. And more. Why still so high? Ah, coming down, but from a height. This might hurt. Surely no bounce this time. Hit again. No bounce at all. More of a thud. There was a bush to one side, and gorgeous wet grass with soft earth beneath it. What a flight. What a landing. What joy.

'Everybody all right?'

'Yes,' said two Dutch voices.

'Good heavens. Where is Geoffrey?'

'He is not here,' they said.

'Well, where is he?'

Looking for a whole man around three sides of a basket and all sides of a bush has a touch of fantasy to it. There was nowhere else to look.

'Geoffrey?' I said, querulously, having no idea how loudly to call, 'where are you?'

The Dutch pair started looking under things, under the map, under a sandbag. They looked most serious.

'Geoffrey,' I shouted, less loudly than before.

And then he appeared, fifty yards away, behind an embankment on the far side of a small canal.

'Why, hello', I said, greatly relieved, and the Dutch couple put down the map box they had been searching.

Apparently he had fallen out at the first bounce, thus causing our rapid rise. The cameraman then showed me his broken Arriflex and the haphazard result of both mishaps was to restore my faith entirely

We ordered our balloon. It was made by Albert van den Bemden in Brussels. In his house the fabric and the net took shape. Baskets were another problem and we used veteran objects of dubious strength until a Guildford firm brought us more securely up to date.

The necessities for a balloon flight. They amazed us in the early days with their variety, their weight, their complexity; but, given this assortment of oddities, it is possible to take to the air with a sizeable proportion of them. Afficionados will be able to detect (roughly from top to bottom) support vehicle, filling tubes, balloon fabric, balloonists, basket, telescope, binoculars, national flag, load ring, valve, ground anchor, cameras, film, first aid, net, gas (a token cylinder), spade, trail rope, sandbags (another token number), life jackets, purity meter, valve line, rip line, rucksack, warning notices, torch, compass, gloves, log book, notebook, souvenirs, cups, radio, tape recorder, knife, ice axe, banner, postcards, anemometer, licence, passport, instrument panel, champagne and food. Not all are 100% essential, but all contribute from time to time.

29

Alan and Joan Root, naturalists and film-makers, joined the balloon safari on its arrival in Africa.

in the business of ballooning. Some of the others were still airborne, still travelling further to the east, and they waved and we waved, and they looked magnificent. I thought then, and still do, that a flying balloon does have a perfection to it. There is a sort of majesty to the event, however ludicrous its associations, however idiotic its aftermath. The cowpat on the landing site merely highlights the previous excellence and makes it all the more remarkable. A flight by balloon is like no other.

Therefore it was Dongen that resuscitated Jambo and breathed new breath into me. That night, at the so-called *Diner des Survivants*, I found myself incorporated within an extremely modest band of practising balloonists. Their whole sport was a survival and they pursued it with a mixture of nostalgia for the past and of love both for the flying and, possibly yet greater, for the ground festivities. The greatest *ballonfest* of the year is that of St Niklaas in Belgium and it lasts for three days. The actual flight probably lasts for thirty minutes because the dozen or so balloons, having taken off unforgettably from the town's cobbled square, suddenly have to remember the Antwerp control zone. The wind customarily blows everyone in its direction, and every balloon has therefore to be landed short of the zone's frontier. On the years when unfavourable weather prevents flying, the festivities are equally gay or possibly gayer owing to the greater quantity of time not taken up by the labours of inflation, take-off, flight and subsequent retrieval. The sport of ballooning is more open-minded than most.

At the Dongen dinner, as the courses were set before us with that undemanding haste of the Continent which transforms a meal into an evening, I got to know the leading members of the European fraternity of aeronauts. The strangest realization, which hit me during the ninety minutes closely sandwiched between the end of the meat and the start of the dessert, was the general age of my companions. One might have thought, with a sport demanding the perpetual lifting of 40 lb. sandbags during each inflation in preparation both for the flight and the eventual turbulence of every landing, that I would have been surrounded by youthful gymnasts. Failing that, the assortment should have been of powerful giants who could treat the sandbags with as much disdain as the rough and tumble of hitting the ground at 30 m.p.h. As it was, the man sitting on my left, the most experienced of them all, was well into his seventies and had a physique much like a bent twig. His clothes fell about him uncertainly, not knowing from which particular projection of bone they should be hanging. His frailty was the most enormous thing about him, and it had not been helped by two motor crashes.

Nevertheless, in his own fashion, he was a tower of strength. He ate enormously. Steaks seemingly twice his size disappeared effortlessly without any increase to his own bulk. No course was refused or pecked at. He never went early to bed. He was never late at early risings. He was a Frenchman but he spoke both English and French breathlessly, as if his thoughts flew along too fast to be converted into mere words. His enthusiasm for lighter-than-air activities was absolute. His youthfulness was ageless. His name was Charles Dollfus.

I sat there that Dongen evening listening to his stories. He could compare the excellencies of travelling in the Graf Zeppelin with those of the Hindenburg. He knew people like Henri Farman and Louis Blériot, the unsuccessful and the successful contenders for the first Channel flight. He could describe Albert Santos-Dumont, the zany little Francophile of a Brazilian who spent his coffee money on a succession of airships and aircraft, and who landed them for some time almost exclusively in the built-up area of Paris. Dollfus was the first aeronaut of any kind to arrive at the smouldering

remains of Britain's R.101 lying across a wood and a field on the Beauvais hillside. He was more responsible than any other person for the creation of the Musée de l'Air, the world's best assortment of aviation bric-à-brac. He took part in the Gordon-Bennett races, those international rivalries between the wars when balloonists ascended from a spot like Brussels with a west wind behind them and the entire Eurasian landmass ahead of them.

In fact Charles Dollfus has more lighter-than-air flying experience than any other man alive. His first visit to Britain was by accident and by balloon. A normal flight in western France in early 1914 had been overtaken by a powerful wind, and this had sent him out over the Channel. It was soon night, and at daybreak he came down for a landing. Reasonably enough he hailed the first people in English. Less reasonably, or so he felt, they answered in a yet stranger tongue. There was then a lot more talk on both sides, but each group, those on the ground and those up in the trees, remained equally uninformed about the other. Eventually the men below managed to pull both basket and balloon down from its perch and Charles Dollfus realized that he had landed in Wales.

Fred Dolder had a little white beard, a stockier frame, and was also elderly. He came from Switzerland and did much of his flying over the Alps. At a time when other men might be giving up bowls, he started the High Alpine Dolder Ballooning Week. This is a concerted assault upon Europe's highest mountains by anyone with both a balloon and some sponsor to pay for the gas. (It costs more at the altitude of the best launching points.) Some extraordinary flights

The African flights were astounding in every way, beautiful, frightening, awesome, spectacular, lyrical. The crew were usually Anthony Smith, Alan Root and Douglas Botting, but it was the pilot who was responsible for keeping the serenity of flight (right, over the Athi plains) as prolonged as possible (overleaf top, above Lake Manyara) until the inevitable took place (Saleh forest).

have resulted. One went over the Garmisch stadium with its occupants regretting that they had not landed within it – until the wind reversed itself and they were able to do so. Another balloon was suddenly caught in a vicious updraught, and only became stabilized at 25,000 feet. It may even have gone higher because the barometric needle went off the scale at 8,000 metres and only returned to that point an hour later. Anyway the two occupants complained of considerable weariness but, without any supplementary oxygen, were sufficiently conscious to maintain their log correctly every quarter of an hour. Fred Dolder, having despatched every other pilot safely to their transalpine destinations during this annual festivity, then launches himself. His crew-cut crop of white hair ascends once again into the snowy world now so intimately connected with his Dolder week.

Jo and Nini Boesman, the Dutch couple who ballooned off on their honeymoon, run the active Haagsche Ballonclub but they travel elsewhere for much of their flying. A balloon anywhere is a fairly bizarre sight, but the Boesmans have flown in Lapland (no electricity, no control zone, no night), in Haiti, Surinam, Czechoslovakia, Israel, Java, Rhodesia. They help to make it pay by producing decorative envelopes, aptly embossed and correctly overprinted to be a marketable commodity. That Haiti flight even caused Jo Boesman's likeness to be on the stamps themselves, but all envelopes – or covers as philatelists call them – that have flown by balloon are thereafter posted, preferably near the point of touchdown, and have a value greater than the cost of envelope, stamp and labour. Or so it seems. One man, who had brought an exceptionally attractive girl to a balloon gathering, explained that she had come along to lick stamps. Immediately dubbed Fräulein Stamplich by the English community, she did spend a very considerable amount of time living up to her explanation.

Albert van den Bemden, who had made Jambo with the Schaut family, alleges each year that he will give up the sport but he seems to accumulate a greater passion for it with the triumph of each flight. I think he is the most cunning member of the fraternity. While I have been struggling to maintain equilibrium at 500 feet, he has been some 480 feet below me almost planting each handful of sand on the rooftops immediately beneath him. 'What's Albert doing now?' we would say as he either leapt up to catch a wind or descended to slip along obtrusively between the complex furnishings of the ground. He was also everyone's handyman, always ready with glue or valve grease or break-thread or cord, but having helped others to get airborne he then proceeded to beat them in the race. 'Where's Albert? Oh there! Well, that is where we should be.'

Alfred Eckert, a Bavarian, probably flies more frequently than anyone else in the business. He works with a printers in Augsburg, but makes powerful use of an arrangement with a chemical works whereby some of their waste hydrogen is piped directly to a field known as the Ballonplatz. Such a bonanza of instant gas is a balloonist's ideal, and Alfred is quick to turn on this piped dream, to float away from Augsburg, to reach the forbidding Alps – perhaps, to reach the forbidden eastern border – perhaps, or possibly to reach nothing in particular, to add one more flight to the log book, to amass one more set of photographs. He has flown in the snow dressed as St Nicholas. He has fantastic pictures taken in the clear frozen mountainous air above the clouds. He has his perpetually buoyant enthusiasm which, coupled with that bountiful gas, sends him up at the glimmer of any opportunity. He even signs his name so that it ends up in the flourish of a balloon's round shape.

Generalizations are impossible about this very special community. An outsider might find parallels, but I could never see any, save for the love of silent flight which afflicted them all. Ben Steeman, the pipe-smoking lawyer, looked more English than Dutch, and occasionally one or other of his eight children watched as their father

Not all the African landings went unnoticed, and "we walked away from each landing with a growing astonishment at our good fortune".

34

It was an eventful place at all times, whether travelling by land between balloon flights . . .

... or breaking camp in the so-called dry season.

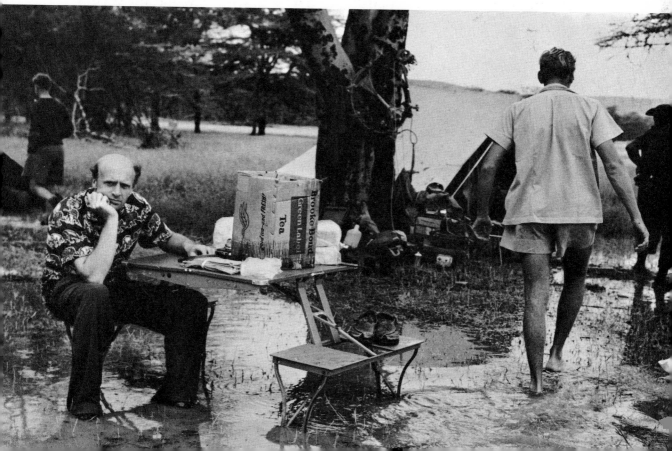

And the animals, whether eland or reedbuck, made it unfailingly beautiful.

ascended leaving them far below. Francis Shields was an American free-lance labourer and builder, who saved up devotedly for one annual series of flights over Europe. These complex, highly social, dual purpose visits came to a brutal end when his balloon flew straight into the Viennese television tower causing him and his two passengers to fall to the ground, still standing upright in their unsupported basket. Peter Pellegrino, another American, normally worked with the problems of air traffic in the most congested skies of them all but, as devotedly as Francis, came over to fly as often as possible in a craft which flew on its own for 120 years before an engine ever pulled man upwards to cause the birth of traffic in the air. A Berliner, Richard Jahre, did not even decide to fly the Alps until he was sixty-eight, but thereafter made it a habit.

There were various others, all aeronauts as they called themselves, and all so different. I was thirty-six when I joined the brotherhood, and felt pleasantly young. Not only was Josef Vanderstraeten, the organizer of St Niklaas, deep in his seventies, but he had the patronage

of the Sax family and every female in this remarkable family plainly stirred even the most ancient of us. It was they who helped us to remember the Antwerp control zone, and to hurry back to St Niklaas, unless we had one of them on board. Then, poised 1,000 feet above the Earth and having champagne poured from a silver goblet by, say, Jacqueline, it was hard equating life with such a thing as a control zone. Fred Dolder always said he was reborn during a balloon flight. Others, less demanding, were overtly content to be rejuvenated.

From the Dongen flight, much inspired by my distinctive colleagues, I returned to England with Jambo's basket on the roof and her bulk in the boot. I was enthusiastic to return, to fly again, to put further healing tissue on the African wounds. It was a shame there was no ballooning in England, but the Continent was so near and its countryside and people added an extra dimension to the sport. To fly over Bergen op Zoom, or Waterloo, or Arnhem, or even Zutphen (how on earth could Philip Sidney or anyone else have been short

of water in that bewilderment of snaking streams?) plainly had advantages over Swindon or Scunthorpe, and the flatness of north-western Europe is undeniably satisfactory for the perplexities of ballooning.

On the way back to England we argued over the reasons for ballooning, and why such a curious mixture of individuals felt so elated by the sport that they were prepared to amend their lives for weeks at a time to savour more of it. After all, their enthusiasm had to be intense to compensate for the effort involved. Some had to drive several hundred miles to reach the take-off point and they all had to work extremely hard for about four hours before the inflation was complete. They then flew high or low over the countryside in a craft which, however meritorious the system, could kill its occupants with an immediate savagery. Finally they landed, crudely or casually, in a distant field and had all the problems of packing up that gear, transporting it to the roadside, waiting for the recovery party and driving back to base along the man-made confusion of roads over which they had floated so peacefully throughout the afternoon. It was an exhausting hobby and an expensive one. It was ludicrous and dangerous. It was an extraordinary mixture of the desirable and the unwelcome.

The danger was obviously important. In the first place the aeronauts all knew people who had been killed in the ballooning business. They knew of countless others who had refused to step into the basket and who had stated, quite bluntly, that they were too afraid to do so. They knew of passengers who, after expressing a willingness to fly, then spent the entire flight crouched at the bottom of the basket. However it was obvious that danger was not the aim, and the balloonists were only too happy to avoid its lurking presence whenever possible, to cancel the flight, to take more sand instead of more people, to stay at home.

Nevertheless the danger could not be totally avoided. The hydrogen gas is a tinder box, ever threatening. The atmosphere is totally untrustworthy, ever ready to transform a calm day into a nightmare. A peaceful flight at 5,000 ft. can be overtaken by a stronger wind, and the zephyr present at the take-off can become a gale carrying the balloon along at a fearful pace. Lightning can suddenly arise from the best of days and will strike balloons with disastrous effectiveness. A flurry of snow can freeze the valve and remove all such descent

me we film. Within
Ngorongoro crater
vildebeest produces her
f. Within a couple of
nutes the calf stands
its feet. Within
nutes more the hyenas
ack and the mother
es in vain to drive
m off.

control as the balloonist posseses. Visibility can alter dramatically, leaving the balloonist plotting his position invisibly by listening to the take-off snarls from airfields or the steadier roar of the major highways. The landing is the greatest hazard of them all as the aeronaut permits gravity to win again and tries to decide which piece of the landscape ahead of him is most suited for a return to Earth.

Were all these men seeking this kind of exposure to danger as they drove to yet another ballonfest? Were they thinking of the hazards to come as they donned Edwardian plus-fours, or made idiotic speeches before the flight? Somehow the prospect of danger seemed entirely irrelevant to their antics. No man about to ascend the Eiger, or indeed any major climb or any formidable undertaking, is quite so slap-happy about it as the balloonist who is about to step into a wicker basket and entrust himself to the currents of the air. My belief, as I argued on that occasion, is that the balloonist likes his sport so much that he does it even though there are some dangers. Some other sports, or so I argued with less knowledge and therefore more determination, are welcomed by their participants because there is danger. Of course mountaineers take suitable precautions but would there be the same mountaineers, or as many, if some cunning device took all the danger out of it?

Perhaps the balloonists like the singularity of it. Their tie pins, their ties, their cuff-links and even their visiting cards are all suitably emblazoned with the spherical motif, proving to the world that they are aeronauts and not as other men. A bank clerk who goes shark-fishing once or twice a year becomes a shark-fisherman rather than a bank clerk: his tie, his club and his friends all testify to this fact. A

The most formidable memori were of the flights themselves the contortions of the atmosphere, the narrow escapes from thunder-clouds, the firm feel of solid ground.

his Tanzanian landing, more successful
an most, was conveniently within half a
le of the Great North Road, that
nder ribbon (pictured on page 12 not
far away from this very spot) that
d caused the idea of filming animals
m a balloon. Successful landings, those
necessitating days of forest recovery,
re particularly welcome.

balloonist, provided he can stand the tedium of being asked all the same questions by different people all the time, is also in a different category to the great majority. He has flown in the regions of the air. He has a tale or two to tell. He is an aeronaut and none can say him nay.

However even that does not explain the total addiction of the current crop of continental balloonists. They fly whenever possible. They will travel to other continents. Their homes are a welter of ballooniana. All their Christmas cards are on the same theme. Their calendars give it extra strength. They will meet in the Café des Ballons – if there is one in town. They adore exchanging presents, whether dish-cloths, playing cards or lamp-shades, if there are balloons on them. And every now and then, for flights are inevitably well spaced apart, they take to the air. They shout the same sort of comments at the people down below and, once again, they are in their proper element.

In short we argued lengthily, but had no real idea why these people behaved in this fashion. We had no idea why we were joining the club. Americans speak of motivation as if it were one entity, much like appetite or thirst. Sociologists, after unravelling some riddle of behaviour, like to apply the same answer to all of us. Obviously – and in this we were all agreed as we drove on to the cross-Channel steamer – a generalisation is impossible. The danger must be relevant, either attracting or repelling. The unique beauty must be entirely relevant, the perfection of this form of travel. The camaraderie, quaint and with its own set of jokes, must always be important. Someone once called it the rarest sport in the world. It may well be, and it may seem strange to others, and stranger still when they watch the rituals of the game, but we had all been enchanted by that Dongen weekend and we drank a toast in tax-free beer that it should, by no means, be the last of its kind.

With the African days over, Jambo was retrieved from the last forest and the final night stop was left behind.

Back in England the African trip had to be accounted for by writing the book and completing the films for which money had already been received, and spent. When these appeared they helped to promote a wish endemic in a good many people to fly beneath a balloon. A plaque commemorating an early flight said that the aeronaut had been supported on the bosom of the air, and perhaps the whole business is one great mammary desire to return to some form of amniotic tranquillity. I received a fearful lot of letters from people yearning to experience this new joy without the slightest realisation that an inflammable gas does kill people and that one filling of hydrogen, the most abundant element in the universe, does cost £150 for a four man balloon.

Nevertheless there was a way out. Should Jambo ever fly in Britain, the news would get around about the unwelcome practicalities. The first time Douglas Botting and I saw the ten 1-ton cylinders of gas necessary to fill a small balloon, we spent the rest of the day telling each other how heavy 1-ton cylinders really were, and how many of them were necessary to contain 20,000 cubic feet. The sight had been sobering. I have a belief that no human being can fairly appreciate a given circumstance, however much he imagines it beforehand, until he comes face to face with it. Even then he is inadequate, because earlier prejudice and the five senses can still mislead him, but there is nothing like reality to improve the imagination. 'Great heavens, is that a 1-ton cylinder?', we said to each other. 'Great heavens, so that is what a balloon is, and how it works, and why it works.' I felt my correspondents would react in similar fashion as soon as they saw one. It was plainly preferable if I could show them a balloon, rather than write patronizing politenesses.

By remarkable good fortune Jambo had survived Africa unscathed. Therefore Jambo should fly in England with the minimum of delay. It would put the enthusiasts right in the nicest possible way.

From being very much alone Jambo returned to join the crowd.

CHAPTER 2

To Cardington and Over Alps

So much for intent. The first flight in England proved to be a model of ineptitude. The Nottingham Co-operative Society had decided that an appropriate method of celebrating its centenary year would be to sponsor a balloon flight from the grounds of Nottingham Castle. They had asked me and I had accepted. They would see to the gas, helpers, sand, location, police, fire and local authorities. I would see only to the balloon and therefore felt much relieved at this uneven division of labour. After the organizational turmoil of Africa, it would be plain sailing of a high order to concentrate solely upon Jambo and her individual problems. I looked forward to the day with confidence.

It so happened that the balloon was on the Continent shortly before the Nottingham flight. It was still a foreign balloon and there-

fore the annual papers of registration had to be completed in the country of origin. It also happened that I was on the Continent shortly before the flight, visiting Germany. I foresaw no problems. The balloon, so they said in Belgium, would be arriving in Harwich with days to spare. I therefore planned to arrive back with one day to spare and I left Bonn, an easy place to leave, in good order. Meanwhile a steak tartare, rich in its uncooked promise, was sitting in my stomach and biding its time. In London, almost casually, I telephoned Harwich for confirmation. Instead I received total assurance that no balloon either had arrived or was due to arrive. My system contracted, and I put down the phone. With infinite finesse the steak tartare chose this hour to strike.

Take-off was due at noon on the following day. At noon on the following day I was in a London marshalling yard still sans balloon and sans all customary equilibrium. It had not been easy driving to Harwich, inspecting every warehouse, pouring fistfuls of money into phone boxes, checking with Belgium, extracting sixteen-figure document numbers, driving back, speaking with the railways and visiting the stations, while that infamous raw dish kept up its onslaught. To find the right goods yard was a kind of triumph. To see the basket through a crack in the truck was another. To be told that no trucks could be shunted or unloaded after noon on Saturdays was

Suddenly there seemed to be balloons flying all over the world.

the end of the line. Dejectedly I rang Nottingham, and confessed failure.

And then it all began. Nottingham called the railways, and the station responded. That truck door was opened. A trolley received Jambo, and I signed some paper. I brought round the car. On went the basket and in went the canvas sacks. Away I went and headed north. Quite what had happened, or how, I never found out but merely drove at all speed. Soon it was Nottingham, first the city and then up to the castle. Some gates opened. In I sped.

'About bloody time,' said a ten-year-old voice from somewhere.

It was 4 p.m., precisely four hours since take-off should have occurred. The crowd, fantastically, was still there. So was the ground crew, and they worked superbly. The gas poured in and, a mere $2\frac{3}{4}$ hours after my arrival, Jambo was 55 feet taller and swaying all ready to go. I made a brief speech of apology with someone's megaphone, and remember only the very apt, loud replies from the same ten-year-old. Partly to be rid of him but largely in the haste still to make amends I soon cast off and the four of us shot up to 1,000 feet. With great good fortune we flew straight over the Nottingham Co-op, a building suitably bedecked in papier balloons. From that moment on,

One way and another the African trip had to be paid for.

And the European fraternity welcomed the new arrival to their ranks.

soothed by the refreshing excellence of this form of flight, I started
to enjoy the day. Besides the venom of that tartare had suddenly lost
its crippling authority. It had to, up there.

On board were two of the men responsible for the flight and Charles
Dollfus, that exuberant egg-shell of a man. It was my fifteenth flight
and only my eighth in charge. He had over 500 but he kept all
criticisms to himself.

'Ah, but how I love ballooning', were his first words when the
countryside started to unfold beneath us.

He told us that the one major regret of his life had been his failure
to travel on board the Graf Zeppelin when she had travelled from
Germany via Tokyo and the United States to reach Germany again.
The breadths of Europe, Asia and North America had unfolded
beneath her on that fantastic voyage around the world. Flying in the
cramped, high-altitude cabins of today's subsonic missiles, when
boredom, alcohol, doll's house food accessories and other people's
elbows make the most lasting impressions, it is hard to imagine the
luxurious joy of flying in those enormous airliners of the past. They
did have promenade decks and sun lounges. They had restaurants
with wicker chairs. They sometimes had someone tinkling on an aluminium piano. They certainly had windows which could be opened
or closed, and everyone went to sleep in a bed. Beneath them the
countryside did roll by, not an invisible seven miles below but a

pleasing distance away like two or three thousand feet. For a long time the most popular route was Friederichshaven to Rio de Janeiro, non-stop. To arrive at Rio in the night, to float above it waiting for the sun, to watch the new day find its way through all those granite hills to the red earth beneath was, said Charles, 'enchantment'.

Perhaps the airships will come again. Perhaps the very business of travel will be able to reacquire some of its old delights. The airlines are well aware that the sardines they carry are only too happy when the journey is completed and that a well-oiled sardine is probably less likely to complain. The occasional geographical excitements, such as the Sahara, the North Pole or the mountain ranges, are given cursory glances and the plane may lean gently over as its shifting cargo decides to have a unanimous look from one side's set of windows; but, for the main part, the view is given as much attention as it receives on the underground. Life begins again when the engines have stopped and the passengers feel the draught of real air revitalising their systems.

How much better an airship would be. How infinitely preferable as the châteaux of the Loire valley passed pleasantly underneath. Think of the Nile, not as a ribbon snaking along 35,000 ft. lower down, but as a living river, giving up its smells and warmth to the air above, crowded with boats in the cities, pouring life into the fields, meandering through Nubia, vanishing into the Sudd and emerging again on the other side. Each journey of that kind, wonderfully afloat above all the rigours of land-based travel, would be wholly satisfying. Meals would be a distraction instead of the only points of punctuation in a

Back in England people wanted to see this 'safari' balloon and,
best of all, to be taken up in it on a captive flight

timeless existence. Admittedly the airship would always take longer, cruising at a mere 100 mph or so, but its passengers would arrive refreshed instead of simulating the limp leaves of lettuce they folded around their plastic forks a couple of hours beforehand. People would even travel for the sake of the journey and not, as on any crowded bus, for the sake of arriving more speedily, however disagreeably, at the other end.

A trouble is that the airships acquired a bad name for themselves by their monumental crashes and their extraordinary history. Although the Germans had been flying them before the first World War it was their ability as a machine of war that so impressed the world. When four people were killed at Lowestoft, victims of puny bombs dropped by a Zeppelin, the airship's reputation took a savage leap. Even when tracer-bullets had been invented, and so had aircraft powerful enough to plant these igniters where the results could not fail, people still had a fearful regard for the leviathans of the sky. After the war the major nations scrambled to possess them and the subsequent disasters make chilling reading.

Even so, in an age when aircraft can – and do – kill a hundred or more at a time, it should be remembered that airships flew scheduled services for about 30 years and only killed 14 fare-paying passengers throughout that time. The most spectacular crash of all was that of the Hindenburg, so suddenly alight from stem to stern, but about half of its human complement survived that holocaust. Fate is not so kind to the victims of modern aerial disasters. Perhaps the sheer weight of them has made us more immune and we accept the statistics mutely. Certainly we have no right to mock the 'gas-bags' as if they alone were unworthy of caring properly for our lives. The Graf Zeppelin flew safely well over a million miles and with hydrogen in her hold. How much better the airships would be if they were full of inert helium, if their designers applied today's knowledge of metal fatigue to the hulls, and if modern weather-radar could keep them clear of storms. What magnificent flights would then be both possible and safe.

So, talking of airships and the old days, we proceeded north from Nottingham and smelt the sweet smell of a fresh summer evening. Villages came and went. Swifts soared and shrieked beneath us. Round stars of thistledown floated by on their independent courses, and sounds of life and living were wafted up from down below. The air was soft and kind, and we moved along as part of it, without effort, without care and with an enormous feeling of unreality. When the light and the warmth began to go, it was total simplicity in those conditions to land on the trail rope and to finish the flight with its length lying along the ground while we, relieved of its weight, were poised and stationary a few feet from the grass. Two men then pulled our rope to a suitable spot for deflation near the road, and only then did they pull our basket to the ground. By way of modest reward I asked them to climb aboard in exchange for the two passengers, and we then ascended to the full height of the trail rope with someone firmly anchored to its end. Two hundred feet up we stopped.

'Ever flown before?' I asked.

*The invitation to follow in Captain Spelterini's transalpine footsteps
proved irresistible. He had made the first crossing by balloon in 1910.*

'Never been higher than a brick wall', they replied.

All the way back to London, once the packing up was over, Charles
Dollfus continued to talk of the old days in his customarily black and
white fashion. Everyone was either stupid or fantastic. Every aviation
attempt was brilliant or absolute nonsense. (All these words sound
so much more emphatic with a heavy French accent.) Blériot, poof,
stupid. He didn't deserve to succeed. Hugo Eckener, a very great
man. That R.101 was folly, one incredible folly. Lunardi was a liar
and an idiot. Jean Pierre Blanchard was the best of them all, a great
pilot. And then, at about 3 a.m., my seventy-five-year old companion,
the most accomplished aeronaut of his day, fell soundly asleep. I
felt sure he was dreaming of aerostatics. He said he could never
even pass a field without immediately sizing it up as a spot for a
landing.

The Nottingham flight was followed by an invitation to fly from
Swanton Morley. There was to be an air rally plus a steam engine
parade at this airfield in northern Norfolk. I accepted with a personal
determination neither to be afflicted with some Teutonic gastro-
enteritis nor to be quite so laggardly about the take-off time. The
plan was to fly on the Saturday of that rally weekend and then journey,
as ever, to an unknown destination. Needless to say, the Swanton

Morley flight is entirely memorable because of not flying on the Saturday and of journeying to a much loved and well-known destination.

All was going well on the Saturday as the gas poured in through the pipe. Jambo slowly expanded, the sandbags were steadily lowered to accommodate the increasing bulk, and no unruly wind was slapping at the fabric. I watched the round inflation sleeve, and then its roundness slowly sank to a flat nothingness. There was a shout, and the shout said the gas had all gone. The balloon, blatantly, had need of more.

An hour after the talk had stopped, the truck had gone back to London to fetch some more and the flight had been postponed until the following day. This involved certain preliminaries. Every sandbag was hooked on, and the balloon was made as secure as possible. A stormy wind finds a balloon to be both a huge obstacle in its path and one that will yield if a sufficient gust is hurled at it. A balloon leap-frogging downwind, following successive gusts, is a curious sight. Unfortunately it is no mere tent snatched away by the gale, but a thing of gas which will in all probability set fire to the first obstacle in its path, be it a barn or a house, or something greater or smaller.

So we found a caravan and planted it upwind of Jambo. From this I and a friend kept guard, ready to pull the rip cord and release all

The Second High Alpine Ballooning Week was to be held at Mürren in the Bernese Oberland. This meant that everything, gas included, had to arrive by funicular and the balloons were laid out in that superb mountainous setting.

Mürren is perched like an eyrie on the cliff edge. Its height above sea level means that a balloon taking off from its only flat surface is already well on the way to the kind of height necessary for an Alpine crossing.

the gas if need be. During the night, to simplify matters and permit sleep, Max Woosnam and I attached a rope directly from the balloon to an alarm device within the caravan. Should a wind cause Jambo to move and this rope to tauten it would also cause an awakening cascade of tins and objects to fall about. Heaven knows what diuretic brew Max had been drinking that evening, and heaven must also know quite how many times he reached the door to the tune of that alarming cascade.

However haggard we ourselves looked in the morning, the balloon looked well and quite unmoved. The gas truck arrived and we stood Jambo, so to speak, on her feet. Only when the ring and basket have been attached does a balloon assume the proper outline. No one can get excited about a sack, three-quarters filled and well bagged down. No one, or so I also believe, can fail to be moved by a balloon ready to be off. The proportions are so right; the gentle swaying so perfect.

The departure from Swanton Morley should have fulfilled these imaginings. On board, shortly after take-off, it was marred by the snapping of one of the eight ropes between the basket and its supporting ring. The other seven appeared satisfactory, and the flight continued. There were four of us: myself, and Mary West, who had been the London-based and delectable secretary of the African venture, and two V-bomber pilots who had suddenly materialized at Swanton Morley. They liked the idea of such a volte-face in their flying experience. Anyway the four of us and the seven ropes all flew south-west, and the sun shone brightly over that Dutch area of eastern England.

One hour later, when the pencilled line on the map showed our course rather more precisely, we were plainly heading for Bedfordshire in general and towards Bedford in particular. The idea then arose that we should land at Cardington. Its old airship base, the point of departure for the R.101, was a most apt destination. Jambo's basket had come from its store-room, and it would be good to land that same basket on the green grass of what was left of the Cardington field. Admittedly the two vast airship sheds, the gas-holders, the stacks of cylinders, the barrage balloons and a meteorological tower made the field more cluttered than most, but the idea was irresistible.

Essentially Mary served drinks and produced sandwiches while the three of us plotted how best to arrive at Cardington. The flight had lasted for one hour when we had had the idea. There was then,

The mountains are ll around, but they re attached to 1other world. Their e, their avalanches 1d their rocks are wwerless, and it is a 2licious experience to il scornfully past 2em."

57

assuming a reasonably constant wind speed, about two and a half more hours to go before it could be fulfilled. A balloon, of course, only travels with the wind, and can no more fight against the wind than can a cloud or thistledown; but a balloonist can choose which particular wind suits him best. In the northern hemisphere the wind at 3,000 feet is travelling at about 30 degrees to the right of the surface wind. The intermediate heights, according to this general adage, have winds travelling in correspondingly intermediate directions. Therefore, assuming the flow of air over the land is behaving according to the book, it is possible to steer a balloon – within limits – by going up or down. The limits are those 30 degrees.

Such a small arc of choice is quite large if chosen in time. Viewed from Edinburgh most of southern England is within 30 degrees, and much if not most of the south Atlantic. Viewed from northern Norfolk all of Bedfordshire was within our grasp but we were only interested in one heavily obstructed field within that general compass. Therefore the plotting of our route had to be very precise indeed. This meant a complete dedication to map-reading. It also meant estimating the wind direction both below us and above us. Below us the smoke and the corn were positive indicators. Above us there were the small puffy cumulus clouds of a summer's day, and their shadows on the

Jambo took off in company with Circus Knie and Tropi. No balloon was fully inflated because the gas would expand following the necessary rise in altitude.

Douglas and I took off first, and watched the other two climb beneath us.

ground showed us the direction in which they were travelling. Our own direction, intermediate between high and low, was provided for us either by the map or by our own shadow. This not only seems complicated, but was so. Mary poured the soothing drinks.

A to B was a firm line drawn on the map from the first fixed point of our idea to Cardington. If we were to the left of that line we had to ascend, and we had to descend when to the right of it. The smoke and the cloud shadows provided the necessary yardsticks, and of course these were never constant because the atmosphere is such a tortuous interaction of innumerable forces. Nevertheless the broad pattern existed, up for right, down for left, and it did seem most magical when the huge Cardington sheds appeared dead ahead. The whole trip appeared even more miraculous as we coasted slowly towards the field, dropping our trail rope on a stack of gas cylinders after crossing the final fence, and then thumping ourselves down into the thick, wet grass. Cardington's basket fell over on Cardington's field and we sprawled into that clover, totally triumphant.

It was a Sunday and the place was extraordinarily empty. The establishment that had witnessed so many lighter-than-air departures had watched our silent arrival with considerable reserve; but we did

Jambo's shadow, so conspicuous initially, was soon to become no more than a dot.

find a man later on, and he did have a key to the bar. As for the basket, so battered by Africa and so plainly in need of replacement, we left its diminutive shape by the side of the 101 hangar and just next to its 200-foot doors. It looked most small, and smaller still as we drove away. They found it in the morning, and kept it for a time, and then they took it out and burnt it when tidying up the place.

The continental experiences, plus the Nottingham and Swanton Morley flights, had restored all lost faith. Ballooning was great. It did not have to be a survival exercise. It was not an aerial roulette, certain to be disastrous in the end. It was indeed safer than angling, as Jo Boesman always said. The invitation to take Jambo to Switzerland for a high alpine flight therefore arrived at a conveniently confident moment. I accepted, asked for details, and started to read about the cisalpine experiences of earlier aeronauts. They all had good tales to tell.

To take a balloon to the Alps is to mix the frailty of cotton fabric and wickerwork with the severe practicalities endemic in mountain peaks. On the one hand is the gossamer delicacy of aerostation; on the other crampons, pitons and the North Face of the Eiger. In fact this apparently contrary mixture of balloons and mountains is

The famous north wall of the Eiger (above) passed to one side and then below us as we slowly ascended and travelled to the east. The instrument panel, with legends added in the light of experience, was a permanent reminder of the hazards to come.

"Below us was the rock and lower still the compressed activity of each Alpine valley, but the zone between this jagged land and the high blue air was entirely fit for a balloon."

Perched over three miles high, with everything under control, and with a miraculous view on every side . . .

entirely harmonious. It is possible to float where aircraft are loathe to go, and to have confidence that the sand at your feet will get you out of trouble, of downdraughts, of clear air turbulence. The mountains are all around, but they are attached to another world. Their ice, their avalanches and their rocks are powerless, and it is a delicious experience to sail scornfully past them. We were even to fly past that famous North Face, to look at its central 'spinne' as we ate bananas, to wonder faint-heartedly where the two climbers were who hung at that time, frozen and dead, upon their climbing ropes. Higher up, the jets whined as they kept well clear of the region. Below us was the rock and lower still the compressed activity of each Alpine valley, but the zone between this jagged land and the high blue air was entirely fit for a balloon.

In August 1963, Jambo was flown by freighter to Basle, driven by Land-Rover to Lauterbrunnen, hauled up by funicular to Grütschalp, pulled by Alpine tramway to Mürren, and then taken by electric trolley to a piece of flat ground in that perpendicular environment. The occasion was the Second High Alpine Ballooning Week. The first such week had been in 1962, and the pilots and passengers had reported back from their scattered landing sites with such exuberance that a repeat performance the following year was obviously essential. The BBC liked the idea of filming and paying for an Alpine flight, and a large group of us arrived at the town of Mürren. This place, perched on the edge of a 2,000-foot cliff and immediately confronted by the Eiger, Mönch and Jungfrau, was the starting point. It stood 5,000 feet above sea level and I think my palms were wet from the moment I arrived there. On each unfavourable day all pilots were assembled for a *kurs*, and on these briefings we were instructed in the techniques

. . . it was occasion to have a snack in that unbelievable situation. Douglas eats the sausages and I the grapes.

of landing on glaciers, on the subsequent procedure, on survival at altitude. The classroom was generally enshrouded in cloud, and every now and then the weather stations would let us know what was happening beyond our particular eyrie in the Bernese Oberland.

One freezing summer evening, as we sat warming our hands on Glühwein, the meteorologists suddenly predicted clarity and a fine wind from the west. Three balloons were to fly, namely Tropi, Circus Knie and Jambo. All three were then laid out, connected to the gas (hundreds of small cylinders had been brought up the funicular) and slowly inflated overnight while their crews had a good night's rest – or so we were instructed in the ultimate *kurs*. Such fitful dozing as could be managed was punctiliously cut short at 4.30 as *Fahrtanfang* was scheduled for 7 a.m.

I met the others and went along the dark pathways in a state of incomprehension rather than fear or excitement. This feeling was still uppermost when it was time to clamber into the basket. Only Douglas and I were with Jambo, for higher altitude means smaller payload, but we had with us two ciné cameras, 2,500 feet of film and a couple of batteries. By the time other extras had been added – food, ice-axes, drink, instruments – there was only sufficient lift for five sandbags. It was generally reckoned, not without excellent reason, that six was the minimum, but Jambo was on the small side for Alpine flying and everyone turned a blind eye to this point. Anyhow, as many predecessors of all kinds must have said as they have climbed into all forms of craft, it was too late to do anything about that.

'It is now start time', said Fred Dolder, the organizer.

'Goodbye', we said, and we went.

Fifteen minutes later that ballast reserve was down to two and a half sacks. The Eiger was still ahead of us and Mürren was 8,000 feet below, but it was necessary to throw out the half sackful to be sure of missing all the peaks in the area. The grey, gritty sand poured down and disappeared in the great wealth of air beneath our basket. The half sack pushed us up to the necessary height and to some 16,000 feet, but this was guesswork because the altimeter had unaccountably not wound itself further than half that altitude. However there was no difficulty in seeing our location precisely because the craggy world below looked extraordinarily similar to its representation on the map. Mürren slowly disappeared behind the Eiger, and we floated east over the twisting Eiger glacier. How on earth could Shakespeare have known of thrilling regions of thick-ribbed ice?

The day heated up and we went up with the heat. It was not cold in that full sunshine but the things hidden in the depths of the basket were strangely refrigerated. We must have reached 18,000 feet, and felt no exhaustion from the lack of oxygen, but we did, or so I believe, suffer intellectually. The ordinary routine of photography, demanding sufficient film, correct aperture, appropriate framing and the right attention to all its various details, proved increasingly difficult to achieve without error. It was easy to detect each mistake; it just happened to be doubly simple to make them. Douglas spent some ninety minutes with his arms in the changing bag, a business of reloading magazines which ought to last a few minutes but took ten times longer. I also found the arithmetic of calculating our speed to be severe rather than elementary, but such a minor idiocy never became the greater stupidity of imperilling the flight in any way. Floating at 20 miles an hour at such a height over such a world sharpened one's appreciation of potential danger, despite a general blunting by the thinness of that upper air.

All new sounds were like alarm notes until their innocence had been firmly detected. All changes, more cloud, less cloud, and all the minor contrary winds were immediate trespassers upon our security. They were considered guilty until time proved them unimportant. A rattle of machine gun fire down below had a devastating urgency to it, and could not rapidly be forgotten or forgiven. (It was a Sunday, and Switzerland seems to go to war on Sundays.) A supersonic jet left me intensively afraid long after its final sound had reverberated for the last detectable time. A realization that the landing lay ahead of us became markedly more acute as the hours passed by.

All balloonists rate their Alpine crossings as the most memorable flights of their experience.

We travelled east. It was always beautiful and the conditions were ideal. We had food and had to film a meal, but it was difficult eating the cocktail sausages and chicken legs. The ballast lasted well, and I was always happy to throw out food to preserve the sand. A champagne bottle went down on to some barren rocks and sent back its pathetic tinkle an age later. St Moritz appeared beneath us, and Italy loomed ahead. It struck us as a good idea to try and make for Italy. More magical drifting, and St Moritz disappeared far, far away. The next valley became Livigno and that looked well for a landing. A thin line of houses flanked an even thinner road travelling north and south, and presumably there were yet thinner wires marching in parallel with both of them. There always are wires.

I pulled on the valve, and thought the opposite side of the valley looked entirely suitable. Down we dropped from our hawk-like station, and were happy at the thought of touching the ground again. It had been five hours since take-off 100 straight miles away. Down we went into that valley at 500 feet a minute, and the striding pylons became plain and then plainer. Down towards that opposite side, and down, when suddenly a wind came from nowhere to blow us upwards instead. Idiotically we were returning along our invisible path, both upwards and backwards. I valved rather more to break through this airstream and slacken the ascent. Livigno's welcoming softness faded away. I pulled harder. And harder. And the descent began again. Douglas filmed and I watched. Certainly no one spoke, but the balloon fluttered with the speed and made much noise. At least we would be landing on the smoother Livigno side rather than the hideously craggy valley to the west. At least we would be landing. The last of the sand went over. And became dust in our eyes. And the ground was there. And our shadow. And Douglas stopped filming. And I think we bounced, once.

I rushed out of the basket and fell about on the net in efforts to get rid of the gas from all that flapping fabric. There were patches of snow, and of grass, and rock. And I fell. The gas all escaped. Nothing had exploded. Douglas remained in the basket with both a twisted knee and one eye full of blood from a forehead wound. The snow helped to stop the flow, and the cut from the camera hitting against his head looked quite clean. Anyhow, with him then hopping about and with me enthusiastically trying to make amends for a harsh landing, we finished off the film by propping the camera against

*Dieter Heggemann and Albert
van den Bemden on their way
from Mürren to Italy.*

How did Shakespeare know, and make Claudio speak, of a thrilling region of thick-ribbed ice?

72

73

rocks. It showed us offering snow-encased champagne to each other, without a care in the world.

The first problem was, of course, Douglas. The second was the dead weight of the balloon. Both were at 8,000 feet, and Livigno was a long way below. Two hours after the landing, Douglas had stiffened considerably and the 600 lbs of balloon had been coerced into neat but solid bundles. Some kind of solution did not come readily to mind. I sat down on a bundle, and was staggered to see a solution come panting over the brow of the hill.

'Guten Tag,' he said. 'Was ist los?'

I took him on a brief tour and, by way of explaining what was 'los', pointed out Douglas and the bundles, and laughed whenever he laughed. Douglas was preoccupied with a major headache, but the two of us more than made up for any silence on his part. Events then moved rapidly.

'Ch'è successo?' said some Alpini breasting the same slope. I took them on the same tour, pointed out Douglas and the bundles, and laughed a great deal.

'Have they got aspirins?' said Douglas.

Men accustomed to rescuing injured bodies from the infinite variety of mountainous mishaps were above such trifles. Perhaps they

Map reading was easy, with the Alpine
world so clearly visible on every side as the
shafts of sunlight struck at it.

After *100 miles Jambo reached Italy and Alfred Eckert took this formidable picture as we descended cautiously into the valley of Livigno.*

were not accustomed to speech of any kind coming from an injured person. Anyhow they bundled him up and attached him to the harness of a man half his size. Douglas's limbs flopped about, like those of some nursery giraffe, and the two men left the scene. They also left the bundles.

Six hours later, with incredible weariness but glowing with the memory of a wonderful day, I encountered Douglas once again. A pretty girl, fair-haired, blue-eyed and round-armed, was giving him tea. He had a bandage round his head, his leg lay on a soft stool and he looked very well. 'This is his sixth cup,' she said with wonder in her voice. It was obviously not occasion to tell of our endeavours with those bundles, of the sweat, of the idiotic polyglot instructions from man to man, of the cart, of its collapse, of its repair, and of our triumphant, hooting, shouting, laughing entry both into Livigno and its very first café. There had been no need to get the balloon through those narrow doors or on to the marble counter, but the wine had tasted all the better for such finalities.

'I think he could do with another cup', I said. She leapt to her feet and looked even prettier.

All Alpine landings tend to be both higher and more abrupt than their pilots had intended.

For the whole of the next day Douglas and I, having despatched Jambo by train, were driven back to Mürren by an obsessive delinquent. He consistently made the 300-mile journey yet longer by driving too fast past the signs to read them. A mountain or two later he realized the error and angrily hurtled us back again around Switzerland's serpentine road system which gains in its contours what it loses in horizontal distance. The same

mountain range stays for a depressingly long time on one's field of view, as it switches back and forth from straight ahead to straight behind and as all a car's mirrors show it rapidly in turn. Douglas and I, now so blatantly earth-bound, relived the previous day's flight with perpetual comment and regretted our inability to travel back whence we had come. What purposeful grace it would entail to land once again on Mürren's winter curling patch, the place which acts in summer as the take-off spot for balloons.

On the following day, with us safely decanted in the right valley, the two of us stood again on that spot we had left. Admittedly Douglas stood unevenly, with one leg painfully bent, and the large plaster on his forehead did not go unnoticed, but it was a great moment. The ground there was extremely ordinary, being a poor expanse of grass, and it was raining at the time, and foggy, but the spot had been ennobled in our eyes. To call it hallowed would stretch the word, but we planted our feet firmly on the place where the earth had let us go, and felt most strange and awed.

CHAPTER 3

Piddle Country

To call the high cost of gas ballooning a miserable circumstance is an understatement. It dominates the activity. It means that there always has to be a sponsor for every occasion. He or they, as the pipers who call the tune by paying £150 or more or less for each filling of hydrogen, can make or mar the occasion. They can be undemanding or totally blinded by their power as pipers. Of course it would be pleasant if an appropriately light gas bubbled out of the ground at convenient locations but it does not do so, and sponsors are inevitable. It is best if the event can be seen their way until the flight, and they are then safely left behind.

Most sponsorship arrives in connection with some festivity of which the balloon is a part. At least this proved to be so as the invitations arrived following the transmission of the Alpine film. Flower shows, air shows, agricultural shows and all those varied forms of English fête occur relentlessly during the summer season, and many of the organizers considered a balloon might be an asset to their activities. At least it would make a change from the Lady Godiva tableaux, the gymkhana events, the jam-tasting and home-made scones, the trampoline experts, and recruiting displays as the Army fires off extremely offensive blanks or the police send their Alsatians against some Michelin of a man. To sign on often meant receiving legal contracts, and the balloonist 'hereinafter known as the entertainer' then found himself in another world.

As like or not, the entertainer is given a roped-off section. He looks anxiously at the motor-cyclists next door who will spend the afternoon driving through hoops of fire, and he prepares himself and his balloon for starting time. Girls dressed in gossamer or lord mayors dressed in blankets open the show, sashes over breasts or chains over chests, rain or fine, goose-pimples or heat bumps. The loudspeakers start their predictable programme, opening with a feed-back shriek and continuing via the entry of the gladiators to talk of lost children, the owner of ECK 910, the arrival of a television personality, 'Give him a big hand, there he is, yes he's waving', then with a heavy click the

82

The date : 1963. The place : Malmesbury. The occasion : Carnival time.

Jambo's presence seemed entirely in tune with such festivities.

tape recorder starts up again to produce the 'Teddy bears' picnic' because someone has arrived with a team of footballing pekineses. It is strange hearing oneself described by these loudspeakers with wrong facts and worse humour and to be impotent with all that noise from every quarter. 'Yes, I can see him. He's picking up a sand-bag, and now he's picking up a steel bar and waving it. Well if it's hot air they're after I'm their man, and not forgetting our publicity com-mittee, and now I see our friend the Mayor and his good lady wife approaching the balloon, so it's time for . . . ', and the tape recorder jumps on to 'Up, up and away'.

The mayor is often the first to have a captive ascent, and his good wife has also to be lifted into the basket, thighs and all. One end of the trail rope is securely attached to the ring and the other to a firm anchor point, like the axle of a car. A group of helpers then holds the the rope and they slowly permit mayor, wife, gossamer girl, a photo-grapher or two, and the balloon operator to rise above it all while the loudspeaker pulls out the stops about losing the mayor at last, wondering who will be thrown out first, and asking with heavy innuendo what the problems might be if they stay up there too long. A round balloon high up on the end of a rope is as unstable a device as any if a wind is blowing. Despite efforts by the key men down below, they are flung about on their rope, and the balloon is flung about, and the mayor treads on the foot of the girl, and the photo-grapher loses his hat, and the loudspeaker goes orgasmic with delight.

The rope-men try to soften the eventual landing but it is difficult both stopping the basket and then grabbing it. It is impossible not to give the commentator further joy, but even he restrains himself as the mayoress tries to manoeuvre her frame through the ropes while the balloon topples from side to side. Captive ascents make one suspect that clowns paint a grin on their faces, before being sub-jected to some punishingly comic turn, because that is the only way to keep one there.

If the wind permits, and if others wish to repeat the mayorial performance, or even pay the organizers for doing so, more captive flights will take place. On a good day they are fun and on a bad day they are horrific, but on any day they have a frustration to them because a balloon is nothing if not floating free with the wind. Eventually the time for departure is near enough to call a halt to the captives, and the most suitable ballast at hand is always a basket full

of people. Despite the impression given by the afternoon's junketing, a balloon is a flying machine which can both break governmental rules and kill people. Therefore it is necessary to get a good met. report, to find out wind facts and lightning risk, to warn downwind airfields of one's imminence, to take note of forbidden zones and danger areas, to study one's probable track on an air map, to become a pilot and stop being a clown.

It is also necessary to sort out one's flying companions. Jambo's total lift, when full to the brim with hydrogen, was about 1,800 lbs. When the weight of fabric, net, basket and so forth was added to the weight of sand ballast considered necessary for an ordinary flight, the total lift available for the payload of people was about 725 lbs. Thin friends were therefore best. Fat friends or fat sponsors reduced the basket's complement by their own individual bulk. Jambo's capability ranged from two people, when Douglas and I flew at 18,000 feet over the Alps, to six people whenever a suitable bunch of lightweights flew over England virtually at sea level. Lightness was always an asset and provided a totally valid argument as one exchanged some bulky male for his slender companion. The very old and the very young are generally lighter than average but the old are brittle and the young can have anxious parents. Even so, in her time, Jambo carried people from eleven to seventy-five, and the only injuries ever sustained were to ordinary, fit and youthful adults. Perhaps one took greater care when carrying the more vulnerable cargo.

Having chosen one's passengers, or having had passengers thrust upon one, they were made to replace the human ballast waiting patiently in the basket. Then, with as little ado as possible, with the loudspeaker having its last crack of the whip, and with maps and

Whether taking a 75-year-old lady from Fittleworth, or dressing up to look like oddities in any age, it was always the sponsor who called the tune.

instruments to hand, it was only necessary to find one's point of equilibrium. A sack overboard, half a sack, a few handfuls and the whole 1,800 lbs of balloon, ballast and people hovered magnificently above the ground. The wind slowly gathered this new thing into its grasp and the movement of the flight would begin. A few more handfuls of sand and it would go up as well as along. The inevitable trees downwind had to be cleared, but that is always easy with a gas balloon, and then it was time just to watch the retreating scene down below. There was the circle we had left, the old umbilicus of a filling tube, the ring of upturned faces, the greater ring of stalls and tents and the whole world of the English scene.

There was also, on occasion, the complex addition of permission to fly out of an aircraft control zone. 'Hello Gatwick', said the man on board who had arranged this privilege. 'This is . . . Who are we?'

'Golf Alpha Victor Alpha Tango', I said, for the controller's world likes to abide by its own rules of nomenclature.

'Oh yes. This is Golf Alpha Victor . . . oh yes Alpha Tango. We have taken off.'

'Alpha Tango, Roger and congratulations.'

Later on that flight came the landing and a further need, not unreasonably, to call Gatwick.

'This is Alpha Tango again. We are about to land.'

'Alpha Tango, Roger,' said the voice.

'Alpha Tango, actually we didn't, we bounced, and are flying again.'

'Alpha Tango, Roger,' said the voice again.

Its owner then obviously had thoughts, and felt he had better allay concern.

'This is Gatwick Tower. Alpha Tango is a balloon.'

'Gatwick Tower, I was wondering,' said yet another voice, presumably the captain of a VC 10 or whatever, who had been descending calmly from 35,000 feet and East Africa, and for whom the bouncing of aircraft was a thing deep in the past.

'Gatwick, this is Alpha Tango again, and this time we are safely in a hedge.'

'Alpha Tango, Roger and out,' replied Gatwick Tower. The airline pilot said nothing this time but must have had some thoughts all the same as he manoeuvred his own aircraft laboriously over all hedges to touch down on his only form of security.

mpstead Heath, London. A
liant summer's day. An
rely harmonious scene in an
rely harmonious setting.

There is nothing quite like a balloon take-off. One moment you are swaying on the ground and enjoying a final joke. Then, silently and simply, the wind takes hold of you and it leaves the people behind. Soon they are specks and the house itself slips slowly into its setting in the midst of Oxfordshire.

Can there be a better way of seeing this planet, this land we live on and yet so rarely see?

On these British flights the balloon had to be made to obey the regulations that apply to all aircraft. It had to fly under the air lanes, over (or around) the active airfields and outside the control zones (except with permission). It could also only fly in the clear-weather conditions applicable to all aircraft with inadequate instrumentation. This meant no flying in cloud.

Once, on a perfect summer's day and a few miles north-east of Shrewsbury, we infringed this rule most inadvertently. There were clouds in the sky, but not one in our vicinity and we could see both the hills of Wales and the murk of Stafford with enormous clarity. Then, rather quickly, both disappeared. Even the ground below became hazy, and then it too vanished. We had been abruptly enveloped in a misty cloud and the five of us stood there amazed by the sudden transformation. The ordinary rumblings of life down below were also blanketed in our silent, sightless world. Michael, balloon-handler and passenger, lifted up his chin as if to shout something and then said, 'Help,' in a silly little voice which entirely summed up the idiotic situation.

Later on I valved and we dropped out of our cloud to stabilize below it. The world of seeing and hearing grew all around once more, and we flew beneath our companion until it disappeared in the general crowd of an increasingly cloudy day.

In theory, as steam gives way to sail, all other aircraft had to avoid us but, in practice, we loathed the presence of these other machines. We could hear them long before they saw us. We saw them jerk a little as our huge orange orb floated into their view, and then we saw them bank round to have a closer look. Of course we waved, and wrote large greetings – of a kind – on available material, and would lower

ourselves down to the treetops, and watch their turns get tighter and
tighter; but it was always most welcome when they veered away to
let the silence flood in on us again.

The only true man-made thing to see in the sky was another
balloon. Malcolm Brighton and I once took off, tied together, from
Dursley in Gloucestershire and that was unforgettable. For a while
the joint flight was ungainly because contrary winds and the slightly
different behaviour of each balloon caused the rope to tug, to slacken
and then to tug again. Soon we untied ourselves but we remained
in a similar piece of sky, sometimes lower, sometimes higher and
occasionally fantastically close. We could talk, or shout, or just
look at the other balloon. A pair or a row even of ugly things present,
by their symmetry, a better appearance than a solitary ugliness. For
the same kind of reason, although one balloon is already enchanting,
a pair of them are yet more resplendent, and particularly so when one
is seen from the other. The Gloucestershire countryside that day,
always so beautiful between its Edge and the Severn, looked all the
better with its patchwork eternity of varied greens set off by one
brightly coloured blob poised effortlessly in the midst of it all.

From some heights, there is no one down below; while from others
people are all you see and hear. There are some wrapped in each
other and in secluded intimacy at the very centre of a standing corn-
field. There are others, facing the sun with their entire bodies,
dazzlingly unaware of the aerial voyeurs chance has brought their
way. There are houses without people but who explode with them,
from every door and window, as soon as an emissary from the street
has hurtled in to tell them a balloon has come their way. Like the
drawing of a pin from a grenade it takes a few silent seconds before the

94

dramatic effect bursts forth. Once, when over the emptiness of south-eastern Lincolnshire, we saw a single house directly in our path. On every side of it were empty fields and we passed over that house not 50 feet higher than its aged tiles. The desire to shout was irresistible. We made a sound that house can never have heard before as half a dozen people bellowed the noise which first came to mind. What then came out of the house was a man, trousers clutched, braces down, boots unlaced. Strangely he never looked up, and so silently we let him be. That isolated house in eastern Lincolnshire then looked smaller and smaller, and yet more lonely, as we disappeared quite unnoticed, slightly to the west of north.

It was not just bare-bosomed girls or bare-bottomed men who failed to look up and then discover the basketful of trespassers upon their privacy. It was virtually everyone. I remember an occasion when we did fearful damage to the top of a tree but only alarmed the man at the foot of it. The fact that we were in the tree was a failure of judgement on my part. We had been travelling low over an orchard, admiring the medieval antiquity of the trunks and branches, and then over a squat barn, made seemingly flatter by the great weight of mossy tiles on its roof, until it suddenly became obvious that a tall tree was in our path. It was a giant of a pear, twice as high as the plums and apples all around it, and I was suddenly certain that we would collide with the giant. I threw out a couple of handfuls of sand far too late, and we instantly became embroiled in a complexity of snapping twigs. From the ballooning standpoint a tree is a soft thing, becoming gradually harder the more its precincts are invaded. It is a splendid

"The tower loomed. The mourners mourned. The disaster approached most effortlessly."

crash barrier, being increasingly resistant with decreasing speed, and we made a splendid crash into it.

There we stayed a while. Each person was too preoccupied with his or her assortment of twigs, each too near at hand for a decent focus of the situation, and no one spoke coherently. Nevertheless there was great noise as old twigs, dry leaves and hard pears showered to the ground. It was within this very shower that a man stood, beating his head as if a swarm of bees had set about him, and we all saw him straight below us. By then all of those on board had freed themselves sufficiently from their individual thickets to see beyond the first blurred twig, and we watched this thrashing man. The balloon, no longer pinioned so effectively, suddenly realized this freedom and extricated itself from that snare of a tree. Up we went, still dropping a twig or two, and out of the shadow of that tree there came that man, also dropping portions of tree as he walked. One thing we did not do was to call him, and one act that he most positively did not do was to look up at the sky. Instead he stared aggressively at the trunk of the tree and at the cascaded remains it had poured on him. We left him staring in that fashion, and flew on silently.

For the main part flying over England was neither a matter of astonishing its citizens nor destroying the peace of its orchards. Instead it was sheer delight. England is not the motorist's perpetual image of congestion, smell, noise and building. It is unbelievably well preserved, well wooded, well loved. It is rolling, soft fields. It is hedges and copses. It is the home of deer, trotting along the lines of

Wavers in Wiltshire (left) and a crowd at Birmingham (right) grouped around the circular take-off area

corn. It is where hares live, and where swans fly, and where pigeons hurl themselves from one bunch of trees to the next. Of course, every now and then, there comes some fiendish thing like the A.40, so raucously cutting through the peace on every side, but for the main part the countryside is peace. It is grouse on the moors so near to big cities. It is the concentric circles of fish leaping in the lakes. It is the smells that ought to be, and it is pleasantly possible to detect a piggery when 2,000 feet above it. There is the feel of a damp wood high up above that wood, and just next door in that piece of sky is the feel of dry corn or green cabbage.

There is no other way, in my view, quite so well made for seeing one's country or indeed one's planet. To float over it adds movement, the prerequisite for this kind of enjoyment. On one occasion, due to what complex of air movements elsewhere I have no idea, we stopped 200 feet above a field in Sussex. Our recovery party, no longer with such urgent haste to sort out the roadwork web of rural England, wandered over to talk to us. There was, I remember, some electricity nearby and a bit of fake Tudor next to a clump of larches, and the field itself was neither worse nor better than the scores we had already flown over that day, but the magic had gone. It was quaint to be up there, and odd to talk to them down there, and they found it comic and so it was; but it was an enormous relief when a wind came and took us somewhere else. The recovery team went back to their cars, and we once again watched the world pass effortlessly and most wonderfully beneath our feet.

Sooner or later the landing always had to be. The ideal spot was a grass field beside a road. It was better still if there were no wires either before it or after it. And the field was best of all if it were neither pock-marked with cow dung nor laced with electric fencing. Balloons land at the speed of the wind. Therefore events happen either at a snail's pace or at 30 m.p.h. (Faster than that and you should not have been flying.) Either there is time to recruit useful helpers from neighbouring fields during the approach or there is occasion only for pulling the rip at the very last moment before tumbling over everyone else's limbs as the basket falls on its side in whatever piece of land the circumstances have selected. People arrive always, and some of the people are surely smoking. Consequently each landing is followed by vehement talk to keep people at bay until the gas has gone. Only when all possibility of explosion or even combustion has

:h haloes are rare and
ays unforgettable.

vanished, and when the balloon is quite flat, can the balloonist himself relax. Once again his balloon has not caught fire and once again the curiously similar assortment of people at every landing happily help to bundle net, fabric and rope and then to carry each to the road.

With the balloon securely put away, it is occasion for the nearest pub. Everyone attends, for everyone has helped. Whether ungainly roadhouse accustomed to a busload at a time, or a couple of sleepy, low-beamed darkened rooms, the English pub is like none other. 'I would like seventeen pints of bitter, ten Guinnesses, seven Cokes for outside, and a Dubonnet.' The drink comes, it slops over, it gets drunk, it is refilled, and the talk is good and loud.

'This is Piddle country,' says the man at your elbow. 'There's North Piddle, and South Piddle, and even Piddle in the Hole. Were you aiming for Piddle country?'

Outside the perfect summer evening melts into the velvet of night, or becomes a thunderstorm, or just goes on and on. Inside it's more beers and sausages and the firm feel of pickled onions. One might have brought the good news from Waterloo or Agincourt, and the talk aims nowhere and gets nowhere. A bell rings, or a gong, or a shout is shouted, and the place is slowly emptied. The assortment of people sorts itself out, and individuals walk away. The pub door is bolted from within and the cars drive off. Was it really Piddle country? And what was the pub's name? Oh well, no matter. Let's get back on to the A.40. A great flight. A quite unforgettable day, and that is how all days should be.

CHAPTER 4

Movies, Airships and Hot Air

The existence of an active balloon within Britain promoted the cause of lighter-than-air flying in wildly different directions. This meant that one's own activities became correspondingly diverse. They ranged from the peculiarities of the film world to the building of new types of craft. Jambo was made to suffer novel indignities, and everything seemed a long way distant from that original wish to fly over the big game herds of Africa. What was a double-bed doing hanging from the load ring, and why did this have to be transported to Woburn Abbey? Why were Peter Cook and Dudley Moore suspended from the balloon, together with the bare bones of an ancient car?

This particular side of things originated with the discovery of Malcolm Brighton. I had a wish to build an airship depending for its lift, not on hydrogen or helium as with all previous airships, but on hot air. I felt it to be a good idea and Malcolm gave up selling needle bearings to work full time on the scheme. He was an engineer who liked pioneering and he saw sense in the Wasp idea, the warm airship project. We advertised for an assistant and Michael Price, picking apples for a living at the time, came down from the trees to join us. Wasp began to assume a shape with commendable speed.

Wasp itself originated as a natural successor to the African flights. They had been all very well, but the lack of an ability to steer anywhere had been just as frustrating as it had been for all the nineteenth-century balloonists. That age had given rise to a host of semi-steerable devices which then culminated in the successful airships of the twentieth century, notably the big rigids and the pressurized blimps. The blimps, sometimes fitted with a keel to make them 'semi-rigids', had a long and successful career, predominantly as naval escorts, but by the 1960s they had been declared redundant everywhere and thereafter flew primarily as airborne advertisements. The big rigids, developed in Germany, also had a long career. During the first world

Peter Cook, Dudley Moore and Jambo doing whatever it was that the script had called for in "The Bed Sitting Room"

war they changed from being a most horrific military invention to an equally horrific but suicidal flying machine. The cause was that invention of tracer bullets and the development of aircraft capable of putting these bullets where they were so lavishly effective. The similarly spectacular disasters of the peacetime rigids put paid to this line of development but it should never be forgotten, at a time when conventional aircraft kill so many of us, that airships flew scheduled services for some three decades and thousands flew in them with comfort, with gratitude and with safety.

I had no wish to repeat, however modestly, any of this earlier history, but to build a three-man ship kept aloft by air heated to 100 °C. Raven Industries of South Dakota had recently developed a new kind of hot air balloon, in which an impressive propane burner continually produced large quantities of hot air to fill a nylon envelope. I had watched them fly a balloon of this kind over the English Channel in 1963, and I called in on Sioux Falls, South Dakota, during an American visit early in 1964 to have a flight in the same balloon. Its measure of control was remarkable. We hedge-hopped in a manner unrivalled by the gargantuan leap-frogging of gas balloons. Its cheapness was equally astounding because a dollar or two of propane provided the heat for our flight, and the whole operation was relatively effortless. Instead of hours with sandbags, it was a few minutes with that incredible flame. I therefore wanted to apply all these merits to a dirigible. Cheap slow flying, no storage problems (the fabric could be bundled into a bag) and no transport problems (the whole lot would weigh half a ton) had, or so I felt, great advantages in a world of increasingly complex aircraft.

So Malcolm and Michael and innumerable friends set to work. The first assembly of all the various parts was at Cardington where our craft, a presentable 125 feet in length, was dwarfed by the immensity of the 101 shed. Unfortunately the old hydrogen pipes were still in the floor of those hangars, and we had to move when the authorities saw Wasp's kind of flame. So where to experiment with 85,000 cubic feet of airship? The answer was an old sandpit, belonging to Ebenezer Mears of Farnham, which had steep sides, good protection, a dry bottom, and sand in every direction. Sand is superb stuff on which to operate, and proved an excellent base for our work as we blew cold air into Wasp, then turned on the burner, then got the hull into the air, then measured the lift, and decided how best

Belmondo, Jambo and others deep in Southern France filming 'The Tribulations of a Chinaman in China

There had once been a balloon musket duel and this became part of "Those Magnificent Men".

to make the thing controllable when eventually in flight.

Reasonably enough, the business of purchasing such sudden necessities as 1,200 square yards of polyurethane-proofed $2\frac{1}{2}$ oz Terylene, as 35 feet of stainless steel $\frac{1}{2}$ inch tubing, as nylon rope, and refreshments for the twenty friends helping every weekend, meant that the Wasp idea became expensive. It was therefore even more reasonable to let Jambo earn some of this money. How right that the Parisian makers of *Les Tribulations d'un Chinois en Chine,* and who wanted a balloon to be poised on the edge of some cliff-top near Chamonix, should help to pay for Wasp. How right that the creators of *Those Magnificent Men in their Flying Machines* should wish to find out about balloons, and thereby assist the three of us struggling deep in our sandpit.

Quite the most enjoyable of these balloon-film activities happened after Shelagh Delaney had altered the ending of *Charlie Bubbles.* Originally its eponymous hero, the rich, sad author with the big Rolls-Royce, had ended up beneath his car to utter some suitably terse comments as his final words. She decided instead to have him take leave of his weary world by setting off in a neighbour's balloon. Whether flying to death or glory or merely to the next county one was not told, and we did not ask as we prepared Jambo for this new role.

The conclusion of the film occurred at a cottage in Edale. The balloon had to take off from there, but first had to be semi-inflated in the background while Charlie Bubbles, his wife and his child played

Albert Finney at Edale when Charlie Bubbles stood on the three of us to take his leave of the world.

out the final arguments. This caused days of frenetic inactivity while key figures of that particular day's shooting were, one assumed, getting on with the show elsewhere. It meant rainy days and misty days and days of glory when the clouds parted to show the valley of Edale in its exquisite setting. It also meant chicken hampers and tea urns and plenty of talk with the film manufacturers, the carpenters and electricians whose laudably direct aim is to make things work upon demand and without fail. Somebody says what is wanted; everybody then works to make it so. The film world may seem to be comic as paint sprayers turn the brownish tints of autumn into a full summer mantle of glorious green, as electricians drive the windmill according to the script and not the winds, as fibreglass becomes Tudor brick, as a whole sewage works springs up overnight where only sheets and tubes of plastic stood the day before. This may all have a touch of madness to it but the film community knows what it wants, and then moves a commendable quantity of heaven and earth to get it. If the chimneys all spew forth smoke upon command, if the car disintegrates on cue, and if the slimy water both looks slimy and yet leaves its swimmers untarnished to do it all again, then everyone is happy. The film makers are lavish in their enthusiasm for success. They are equally forthright in their disgust at any failure.

They will also stretch every commodity to its limits. A balloon becomes unmanageable on the ground if the winds are in excess of 20 m.p.h. This fact is known. The wind then lashes itself into a fury. Strong men are thrown this way and that by the flapping canvas and, as like or not, this is the occasion when a caucus of directors recommends immediate take-off.

'Never listen to them', said a kindly man whose foot had been severed by a helicopter blade during some action photography. 'Only do what you feel it is safe to do. Don't be pressured by them. The film can wait. They can. You can.'

He stumped off on his wooden foot. I heard no more of him until someone told me the wretched news that he had fallen out of an aircraft while filming some further action scene.

Albert Finney was the principal of *Charlie Bubbles*. It was he who had to notice the balloon a couple of fields away. It was he who had to walk defiantly up to its unattended, buoyant, swaying form. And he it was who then clambered in and whose feet trod upon the three of us crouched invisibly at the bottom of the basket. The script called

"It's the noise nuisance that I object to"

for his solitary departure. Reason called for a couple of balloonists to be on board, and the third body was a cameraman who, lumbered with unwieldy equipment, had to spring up to take further shots the moment the ground cameras had stopped turning.

A balloon basket is markedly small even when four adults are standing in their appointed corners. It is ludicrous congestion when three of them are squatting on their or someone else's knees. Albert leapt in, stood happily on whatever bits of humanity happened to be beneath him, and started to remove the restraining sandbags. In theory I was in charge of this manoeuvre. In practice it was like an aircraft pilot uttering terse, countermanding instructions from some commanding point beneath a seat. I peered with one eye through a one-eyed hole a man had made with a screwdriver. I saw a screwdriver-shaped piece of grass looking very near. Albert put out more sand. The grass moved, and then stopped. Albert put out more. Suddenly I saw screwdriver shapes of hedge, then a road, and then some sky.

'Just got to do my acting', said Albert between his teeth.

At 2,000 feet, or so an out-of-focus altimeter inches from my face told me, Albert said we could get up. It took time that getting up. It needed planning, co-operation and foresight, but I was totally unprepared for the sudden intensity of vertigo: one-eyed holes are plainly inadequate. A normal flight leaves most people unmoved by the gradual withdrawal of the land, in that they have time to watch it go. Key-hole viewing is no substitute, and we all shrank back from the unnervingly abrupt departure. Albert on the other hand, and no longer standing on our various feet, was quite unmoved, and spoke warmly of this respite from earth-bound complexities.

We had two flights from Edale. The problems of sunshine and course and rate of ascent were different on the two occasions, and the directors wanted a choice. Part of the deal was that the flights should not be five-minute affairs, and we sailed on with increasing enjoyment. To fly over a sewage works or rubbish tip is a delight. To fly over the moors to the east of Edale or the rolling farms to the south is, as the scientists say, of a different order. The grouse leapt up from beneath our feet, and careered away with their curved wings ahead of us. The sheep scattered wildly as they have done at every incursion upon their simplicity. The heather changed colour in response to every shift of sunlight. The bracken was brown and red and green. The fields were of every shape; their enclosed worlds so different, and yet so full of harmony. Whether we were high or low, whether the world was map-like or we were brushing along the grass, those Edale flights were entirely beautiful. And, which was markedly more important to that circle of a film crew back in the field, and presumably to the supporters of this first Finney-directed film, we deposited Albert safely back again on the ground. Once it was heather by a moorland road, and once it was grass just beyond a well-spiked thorn, but he walked away from both these touch-downs. In the world of ballooning there is no other definition of a satisfactory landing.

Back, then, to the sandpit at Farnham and to Wasp. With the arrival of that particular winter the place started to become water-logged, but this difficulty was only marginal compared with the problems embedded within our airship. The more we achieved, the more deeply we dug, the greater were the set-backs which we unearthed. We stared disconsolately at the reflection of Wasp's inflated hull in the puddles all about us, and saw only too clearly her misshapen curves, her inherent instability. The trouble was partly a lack of pressure

Balloons look well at the best of times.
Occasionally they look even better.

within, and partly a fault of the hot air running from nose to tail and then back again. Both faults exacerbated each other. The more deformed the shape became due to pressure lack, the more air ran from end to end. And the more this instability manifested itself the worse the shape became.

Therefore, or so we argued in that sodden pit, something must reinforce the shape and something else, like a set of baffles, must stop all that inside surging. To improve the shape we introduced nylon tubes and inflated them. To keep them inflated we had to devise ways of mending the inevitable punctures. To prevent punctures we had to keep all sand away from all tubes (and the sandpit suddenly seemed less suitable as a location). When the nylon was finally abandoned we used sewer-men's rodding poles instead. These worked well but only gave Wasp a different malformed shape. Slowly it dawned upon us, or more rapidly if it was raining or cold or wet and windy, that something was fundamentally wrong with Wasp. We were spending time patching up a sinking ship. It was high time we got her out of our pit and returned to a drawing board. It was occasion to think again. It was also high time to earn some more money, and our modest group disbanded. Wasp would have to wait.

We reassembled as a team whenever there was work for Jambo. It was during this time that we perfected the business of retrieval. In the old days, and in the Edwardian heyday of ballooning, each pilot

The Lebaudy replica looked beautiful, and even flew from time to time.

The trouble was those elevators. They caused us to see and to feel far more of Buckinghamshire than had ever been intended.

took Bradshaw's Railway Guide as essential equipment. By plotting his own position plus that of the nearest station, by discovering the next train and estimating his journey time to meet it via horse and cart, he was able to return home without undue delay. The modern technique is for the recovery team to meet the balloon, and to be immediately at hand with the recovery vehicle.

This requires expertise. To begin with, those on the ground used to chase the balloon the moment it departed, to follow every twist of the road which appeared to lead in the right direction, and to end up in farmyards, in streams and all the other varieties of rural cul-de-sac. The balloon, disdainful of all such earth-bound niceties, would sail on most leisurely, to be greeted, eventually, by the travel-weary ground crew. Therefore a better system was devised. Instead of being impulsive to a fault the team would watch the balloon depart, they would take compass bearings of its true course and they would plot the estimated track on a map. This track would inevitably cut across some major road and the ground crew would then drive towards that major road with all speed. At the very spot where the estimated flight path crossed the road they would park the car and then lean back with suitable nonchalance until such time as the balloon came their way. The balloonist, impressed by their calculation, would lower his balloon and shout out his likely destination.

'Meet you at Watling Street', he would shout.

And there at Watling Street they would be as the basket came down, dusting the world, the cars and the fields with sand in the balloonist's customary fashion. Farmers would be impressed if the ground crew informed them that a balloon would like to land on their field in,

WASP was fascinating, expensive, beautiful and fun. Developing the burner (left). Inflating her striped hull at Cardington (top right), attaching the internal rigging (bottom right).

say, twelve minutes time. They might be further softened up by the gift of a photograph or of a book recording Jambo's earlier activities, and they would not fail to be astonished when the same balloon came rasping through their orchard to land on the chosen field right on schedule. If done with suitable aplomb the whole operation was most satisfactory, and left us all wildly astonished at our joint brilliance. The farmer, still standing with that photograph or book in his hands, would either express amazement or, in totally British fashion, express nothing whatsoever as we landed, deflated, packed up and drove away with our own boisterous wavings making up for any lack on his part. One way and another, or so we felt, our lighter-than-air teamwork had started to operate on a higher level.

Such mastery of the subject as we had accumulated was suddenly put to a most awesome test. A film company wanted an old-style airship and wanted it to be flying five months later. The script called for some intriguing tasks to be carried out by this airship, but the opportunity of building such a craft helped to blind us to the difficulties which lay ahead. With a carefree zest we felt that five months and our experience were adequate, that a whole flying machine based upon the Lebaudy designs of 1903 was not impossible, and we accepted.

With that we drove away from the studios and ordered the fabric. The Lebaudy airship had been the first device of its kind to make a cross-country flight of some substance. It had a pointed bow, a less pointed tail, and was generally deemed by aviation historians to have been a success. The fact that it was grossly damaged on three occasions, that it never flew after 1906, and that later aero-engineers never mimicked its pointed design, was all happily forgotten by most historians and also by us as we set about creating the first Lebaudy for sixty years. Of course we went back again to Cardington. Of course we read frantically from the old books. And of course our diminutive team had to expand. We tried to anticipate all future needs, to acquire an engine, propellers, blow-off valves, ballonet fans, rigging, keel tubing, anchor patches, handling guys, rope, instruments, and time was never in excess. It took a month to acquire all the necessary fabric. It took a month for this to be cut and glued in position. And it took just an afternoon to give the hull an air test, to pump it up, to watch its shape fill out, to see that it was without leaks, and then to inflate it yet further as a pressure test. Blowing up

me of the hot air offspring spawned by the American idea of
nging Montgolfier up to date. Bristol Belle (top right), the first
be built in Britain. Don Piccard's Golden Bear and Leslie
ldsmith's Red Dragon (top left) with Jambo at Dunstable.
ndon Balloon Club's London Pride (bottom left) and the Hot
* Group's Jester (bottom right).*

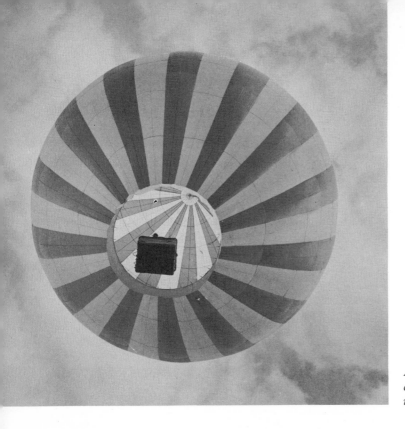

A hot air balloon may look similar when airborne, but there is quite a different ambience in getting the thing off the ground.

a cubic foot of toy balloon can be unnerving. Watching the gauges creep up on something 45,000 times larger, until its membrane of a skin feels almost solid, is terrifying. Just how big a bang would it make should it burst?

That done we then rigged the ship. This meant attaching the hull to a 45-foot keel of tubular aluminium, and then that keel to an 8-foot gondola. This done – another month – the airship looked unbelievably beautiful. The film people came to Cardington. They too liked it. They ordered paint and painters to create a suitably exotic design and then, flatteringly but disarmingly, suggested we built another as a spare. I think we all sat down upon the ground.

Later on we did stand up, and we spent a day or so on the phone ordering more fabric, more metal, more rope, more wire and, above all, more people. The original party of Malcolm Brighton, Michael Price, Giles Camplin and Graham Berry expanded with Barry Wallace and Gerry Long, with Crispin, Paul, James and Denny, with Stephen, Timothy, Darryl and Grant, and it was this swollen group who then lived with the first airship in the piece of Buckinghamshire countryside where the shooting would take place. A huge trailer with Texan number plates stood in a chosen field, and its Texan helium gushed out along our filling tube on the very day that we were scheduled to begin. The airship looked magnificent, with a huge coat of arms on each side, broad bands of purple and white around nose and tail, a brassy keel and a suitably flamboyant gondola. The design was perfect. The airship looked perfect. There was only one snag. As yet, save for some tethered runs within the sanctity of a Cardington hangar, she had not flown.

She did fly. She flew the very next day. She flew on various other occasions, but she never flew correctly. Her greatest inability was to come down. With every manoeuvre she seemed to climb higher. Malcolm had the first flight when a captive run along our field was caught by a side gust and, *force majeure*, he and Giles were aloft. He circled round in conventional fashion to land upwind. He put on more power after the final cross-wind leg in order to counter the wind, and then determinedly ascended irrespective of what he did with the elevators. That flight ended in a pine plantation in the very next valley. Having retrieved our 125 foot of airship, and having tethered it in a field, we then plotted how she could be made to descend. If the elevators were valueless, or so we argued, the whole craft would have to be made to point towards the ground.

A few days later Michael and I were airborne and putting these arguments to the test. At 1,500 feet over the Buckinghamshire fields that we were getting to know so well, he and I coasted along at a happy 10 knots but unhappily ascending all the while. Therefore we initiated the much argued descent procedure. Firstly, we cranked our whole heavy gondola some four feet further forward to bring the centre of gravity nearer the bows. Then we attached sandbags to the bow ropes, and again the airship tilted a few more degrees nose down. Then we shifted all other movables further forward, such as the ballast, the battery and ourselves, until the extraordinarily steep slope of that gondola was more like the crippled Titanic than any airship. Nevertheless, despite this ridiculous plunging angle, the altimeter showed another rise when once more we switched on power. Up there, helplessly climbing and helplessly departing from our homely field, the decks of the Titanic, however awash, suddenly seemed infinitely preferable as a place to be.

We did return, Michael and I. We valved helium to match our inherent ascent. We arrived over our field, and valved some more. We eventually gave a dramatic display of kissing our mother soil when, with unbroken limbs, we stepped safely on to it. There were then further discussions, further modifications and further trials, which did not always return to base. We set off, full of confidence, but minutes later, when a wire had suddenly snapped or a relief valve had stuck, one's mind again had to work with that cold-blooded clarity which comes from nowhere to one's aid.

It was, in short, not a good airship. At least it killed no one. At least it flew. And, at the very least, it taught us a thing or two about lighter-than-air. 'Men of age consult too long, and adventure too little,' said Francis Bacon. We did not consult enough, we adventured too much, and we were all greatly aged by the experience.

Sand is the gas balloonist's perpetual concern. With sufficient he is sufficient; without it he plummets to join all other mortals down below.

CHAPTER 5

Cotswold Continentals

The British Balloon and Airship Club was inaugurated in 1964 within the rooms of the Royal Aero Club. This was only right considering that the original decision to form this aero club in Britain had been taken by three men and a woman when up in a balloon. The decision to form a modern club catering for all the enthusiams of lighter-than-air was mainly a result of Sheila Scott's impulsiveness. It was when she and I were enjoying yet another continental *ballonfest*, and listening to polyglot speeches within the precincts of some moated medieval castle hired for the occasion, that we both felt humbled by the necessity of visiting Europe should we wish to see a quantity of balloons gathered together. Plainly there was interest within Britain. Equally plainly, or so we felt as some burgomaster recounted a ponderously gay episode with a farmer's wife in whose field he had landed, all those interested in Britain should be collected together to meet each other.

There was certainly enthusiasm. About a hundred people came that first evening, and it suddenly seemed as if about a hundred craft would be flying the following summer. Malcolm built the first hot air balloon, using a near copy of the Wasp burner, and a group of

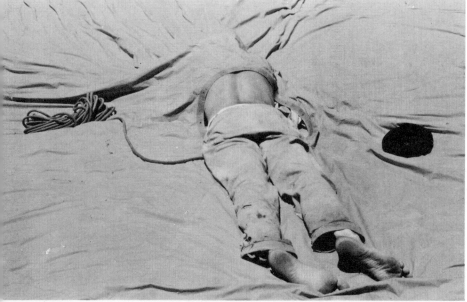

"Let the world scoff at the apparent inanities of ballooning if only it will either fail to observe or not take steps to punish the balloonist's entirely reprehensible errors."

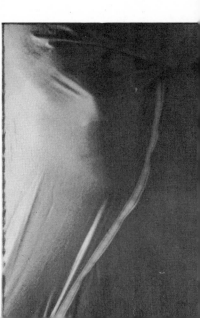

Malcolm Brighton chose to start his check-out flight from Rye to float across the English Channel. It took him, as his mail recorded, exactly 3 hrs 44 minutes to reach the other side.

seven banded together to fly it. Gerry Turnbull emerged from the R.A.F., together with some old R.A.F. balloons which he had purchased, and he signed on with the Board of Trade as balloon pilot examiner. Various groups of students plotted craft made from nylon, or even polythene, and there was also talk of an airship or two. The B.B.A.C., properly established with a list of rules, a committee and a bank account, then undeniably helped to unleash an undeveloped zest for the world of lighter-than-air. Jambo's existence, an easy stimulant of all this enthusiasm, had much to do with the proliferation, however contrary many of the subsequent offspring.

For example, there is a strong dichotomy between gas and hot air. A gas balloon is silent. It is archaic. It is the apotheosis of a dreamlike suspension between heaven and earth. It is, or was, a piece of technology, and yet it seems the converse. It relies solely upon the fact that certain gases weigh less for a given volume than air, and it is only necessary to contain a sufficient bubble of one of these gases to become airborne. A hot air balloon is quite different. To achieve prolonged flight it is necessary to transport some kind of heat-generating system along with the balloon. The convenience of propane (or of butane) is that it can be kept liquid under quite moderate pressures. Therefore no extra energy is necessary to deliver the fuel rapidly to the burner and, by coiling the fuel inlet pipe around the warmth of the flame, the liquid propane is easily vaporized. Two or three million B.T.U.s an hour of heat are achieved very simply, and the firm fat flame soon has the hot air balloonist airborne.

Having fuel vaporized at pressure sounds noisy, and indeed it is. Having fuel inlet pipes, knock-off valves, regulators and pressure gauges sounds a great deal more technological than a gas balloon, and so it is. The tranquillity has gone. The roar of the 6 foot flame

makes speech difficult even with fellow occupants of the basket, let alone with citizens on the ground. The potential mishaps are not the traditional home-spun disasters of fraying ropes or fractured wicker but the sudden severance of a propane pipe. The visible gas, squirting out in every direction, emphasizes most directly the difference between the two kinds of balloon. Each tends to have its devotees. On the hydrogen side is expense, tradition and silence, coupled with the inevitable fear of combustion. On the hot air side is modernity, cheapness, noise and a greater respect for the wind. Both look remarkably similar from the ground, but each type gives quite a different kind of ride. Anyway, so far as the new club was concerned, everything to do with lighter-than-air was to be welcomed, whatever its virtues, whatever the manner of its ascent.

The manner of descent was a somewhat greater distraction for the club in its early days. Do anything, as they used to say in the R.A.F., but never hit the ground when doing it. Club members, in their enthusiasm to get airborne, were subsequently making some remarkable landings. On one occasion, at a Dunstable air rally, Jambo took off and landed well enough at Kineton in Warwickshire, but two other devices made shorter trips. One of them, a superb replica of the original Montgolfier balloon, left the ground with black smoke wisping rapidly from its mouth and landed in the car park. The commentator commentated. The second balloon, a thing of poly-thene strips held together with sticky tape, took off inadvertently when a slender restraining rope proved too slender. Its solitary passenger waved bravely and landed under some electrical wires in a nearby field. The commentator was again in full comment when his microphone went still. The balloon had fused the current and it was quite a time before everyone could be reassured that the un-intended pilot had not met an unintended end.

The club also did not wish to come to a premature stop, and had to create rules and procedures for keeping potentially awkward authorities at bay. Whereas civil airliners can fall out of the sky, and scatter themselves over whatsoever piece of ground happens to be beneath them, we had the feeling that if a balloon ever caused the faintest injury to a third party it would be the subject of a particularly punitive investigation. The sport might even be banned. Therefore it became obvious that the club, more interested in the sport's pre-servation than most, should selfishly look after its own interests by

Inflation and line-up for the Great Balloon Race from Stanton Harcourt.

Fred Dolder, Switzerland

Charles Dollfus, France   *A.S., U.K.*   *Francis Shields, U.S.A.*

preventing foolhardy exercises. In short, if people were to fly balloons, they should learn to fly them well. It should also appear to the inexpert as if we were indeed flying them well.

Unfortunately, whereas a balloon's flight can be just as seriously undertaken as any other voyage, and whereas a victim of a ballooning accident is no less hurt or dead than in any other mishap, the balloon somehow invites mockery. It is a rotund figure of fun, a humpty-dumpty of the air, a piece of light-heartedness deserving to be treated with equal levity. Should a racing car get into difficulties on a slippery track, only the deranged will laugh. Should a balloon be in some equally perilous situation, either tearing free from its moorings or spilling its gas, the chances are that any crowd will have gay hysterics as men are pulled this way and that in their efforts to control their bucking charge.

It is perhaps difficult to appreciate when a balloon is in difficulties. What other craft comes to rest in such a wide variety of situations? I remember landing over woodlands in Surrey and letting the trail rope go in the hope that this would slither over the treetops and thereby help to lower us gently into a field further on. The gentle wind proved to be inadequate and so we stayed there. People came thundering through the wood beneath us but could not see us through the canopy of leaves. They climbed trees and broke branches. They made great noise. They thundered on. So we pulled on our re-straining rope, and edged ourselves towards the field. Eventually we landed in it while the people down below fell about in a muddy

Following the classic "hands off" command, all in their various languages, the balloons take to Oxfordshire air.

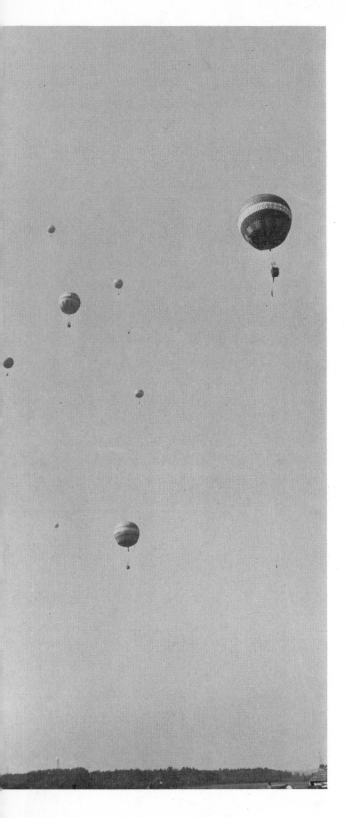

stream between the wood and the field.

'Are you safe?' said someone, himself bleeding from barbed wire and steaming from his exertions.

When impact another time would otherwise have been certain I poured out every last grain of my remaining sack of sand. It got into our eyes. It obscured the view. It was all we had, but it proved just enough to slacken the descent. Instead of our landing in the middle of a twentieth-century electrical cobweb, the wind had just enough time to blow us to the far side of it and there we thumped to earth in the middle of a conifer plantation. Or rather we thumped as far as the trees would permit us to go before they flexed their branches and threatened to throw us upwards. Conifers are better than deciduous trees to land in. Each branch, and notably the growing apex of each tree itself, ends in that suitably stout projection which serves well as a handle. By comparison an oak or a beech ends in such a profusion of brittle bushiness that the discerning balloonist will make for conifers every time. It had been luck this time but we held on firmly and happily to Pinus sylvestris until the entire community of a nearby village came out to get us down. They all spoke so much and so effortlessly that occasion never did arise for telling them of the conflagration which might so easily have been the case.

Perhaps it is just as well that the balloonist's problems are so

Such a sight had not been seen in England for 50 years or more as ten balloons took 26 people to a wide variety of unknown destinations.

128

happily misjudged. He can laugh off those events which others assume to have been hazardous, and he can keep his mouth closed about those frightening times which people merely laugh at. For example, we were once quite high over The Hague in Holland, when something happened to cause an immediate contraction of one's entire nervous frame. Someone inadvertently nudged a 40 lb. sack of sand over the basket's edge. Immediately the balloon climbed higher, but that was of no consequence. With even greater rapidity the sandbag fell, gathering fearful speed as it did so. Down below was all the vulnerable congestion of a major living place, roofs through which our projectile would crash, cars and buses, people in their hundreds, people in their ignorance. Just how many of them was that sandbag going to kill? Very quickly it appeared to have fallen far enough to hit the ground and yet it moved, at least from our stand-point, seemingly horizontally over that city as if seeking out some particular vulnerability. None of the human dots down there turned to look at it, or to run away. The compressed hurly-burly continued noisily, and the sandbag sailed on and on over their heads.

Suddenly it hit a small car park. It exploded on to the ground to make a star-shaped pattern. Not only were there no cars in the six white-lined parking spaces but the bag had hit the turning area. Not a whit of damage had been done to anyone or anything. It was time to breath again, but quite a time before one could laugh again. Later on a man handed in that shattered sandbag to a police station. The hook and the cord were still attached to the eyelets in the canvas, and they thought it might have come from a balloon. Fortunately, or so we learned, they were not sure and we did not go along to enlighten them. Fate had been kind. There was no point in rejecting that kindness, or so we felt, by putting our head in some deserved, official noose. Let the world scoff merrily at the apparent inanities of ballooning if only it will either fail to observe or not take steps to punish the balloonist's entirely reprehensible errors.

This kind of opportunity for pleasant ridicule suddenly reached a new level when the BBC announced early one spring that it would sponsor, and film, the first international balloon race to be held in Britain for over fifty years. It prepared some plastic trophies for the winners. It chose a particular week in May for the event. It picked upon Stanton Harcourt in Oxfordshire as a suitable starting point, bearing in mind the reasonable distance from there to the coast for a

wind blowing from any point of the compass. And, of course, it sent out splendidly gay invitations to the veteran team of foreign balloonists.

Their replies were highly characteristic, totally individual and absolutely the same in that they all accepted with alacrity. Jo and Nini Boesman were to come over from Holland, Richard Jahre and Jo Scheer from Germany, Fred Dolder from Switzerland, Francis Shields from the United States, Albert van den Bemden from Belgium, and the most veteran of them all, Charles Dollfus of France with his team-mate Jean Lesqui. From England there would be Gerry Turnbull, who would fly the 'fox balloon' and of course there would be the famous Jambo. Finally, and out of the blue, came Vic Hunter, one of those civil airline pilots who inform passengers with an equally laconic voice either that the port outer engine has ceased to function or that the aircraft is 32,000 feet over Blackpool. On this occasion he said he wanted to fly a balloon.

We all gathered at a nice riverside hotel on the Thames. The Europeans, each English-speaking to a degree, arrived there full of amazed talk about our road-sign obscurities. Those responsible are to be congratulated that this otherwise competent bunch of linguists were floored by notices of carriageways and seeded verges, of heavy plant and yield and lay-by. Be that as it may they all arrived safely and the Thames punts were soon loud with heathen talk. 'Pas op, Albert. Vorsicht. Nein, auf dein links. Prenez garde. Let op'; but no one fell in.

Came the day. A huge lonely field was the launch site. The foreign team, accustomed to starting places on cobbled squares, football fields or fairgrounds, were amazed at such rustic emptiness, but set to work. The BBC's helicopters buzzed. The ground-based cameramen peered into ground-based activities and suddenly, not seven hours after the first balloon sack had been heaved from its trailer, all ten balloons were ready for the start. Such a sight had not been seen for five decades or more. Such a sight had never been seen at Stanton Harcourt,

Jambo in full flight. On board, apart from the bicycle and cameras, were Joy Hill, Malcolm Brighton, Douglas Botting, Anthony Smith. The orders gave instructions for exchanging passengers.

and the roads clogged with traffic. One farmer opened a field, removed its cows, ushered in cars and charged ten shillings a head. It was a prince of English days, warm, green and seemingly endless.

For some deep reason the race was started on bicycle. A representative from each balloon had to pedal over the uneven turf, leap aboard and take his bike with him. That done he and his comrades could chase after the 'fox balloon', already airborne and ready for the hounds to follow. Jerkily or smoothly, rapidly or in their own gentle time, the balloons moved into the air. It was an unforgettable sight. There were balloons and bicycles on every side, pennants and banners, and through the air came the most multilingual talk ever to have scattered the rooks of Oxfordshire from their elm-top perches.

'Shipton under which wood?'

'No, under Wychwood. Over there. Towards Stow in the Wold.'

'Where in the world?'

The peasants beneath, the makers and creators of this beautiful Cotswold country, heard this chatter and rasped back their own interpretations of where they were; but the balloons sailed on and out of sight quite as mysteriously as they had come. I do not think I have ever seen the land look so well as on that day. The ground was warm. The trees were all so new in leaf. The white Cotswold stone was a perfect piece of harmony with the browns and greens of the land. The sky was a hazy blue, save where it was dotted with the shapes of the nine other balloons. Even the veterans, even Charles Dollfus making his 522nd flight, still speak of that Cotswold flight with a wistful look in their eyes. It had a touch of magic in it, and this will always be remembered.

'Land near the B.4437,' said the BBC instructions, having been transformed into six languages the moment it had been decided which way that day's wind would take us. 'After landing exchange your

PH-BOX, alias Oxygenium, alias Marco Polo, high – and low – over Cotswold country.

t was the day, the locals recall, when balloons fell like apples rom the sky. Jo Scheer (left) making a successful unscheduled top; Nini Boesman exchanging her passenger at the roadside, nd Francis Shields pedalling to complete the journey.

passengers.' In theory this would give the cameras more material at some predicted spot. In practice we all dropped from the sky with the predictability of apples from a tree, grouped in an area but in our own good time, and the cameramen had difficulties. Passengers raced up to the wrong balloons. People raced everywhere. Balloons were everywhere. Mine was in a hedge. It was a holly hedge just one field away from the 4437. We sat in that hedge waiting for our passenger until someone pointed out a major severance along one side of the wicker basket's bottom. There was nothing else to be done, save to pull the rip and drop out of the race.

Very late that night everyone returned to the Thames-side hotel. Charles Dollfus had won; everybody expressed gratitude for the day and also some commiseration for the basket failure. Francis Shields, the American, took longer than most to return after he had seen that a place called Broadway lay near his path, and he too expressed sadness over the basket. So we took it into a field, and we filled it with paper, and we set fire to its forty-year-old, wood-wormed wickerwork. It burnt very well. Its flames leapt high in the air as we all, with flickering faces, stared at it. Its destruction was absolute. Yet there was so much more to come.

Alas for ambition! Structural collapse drives Britain out of the race.

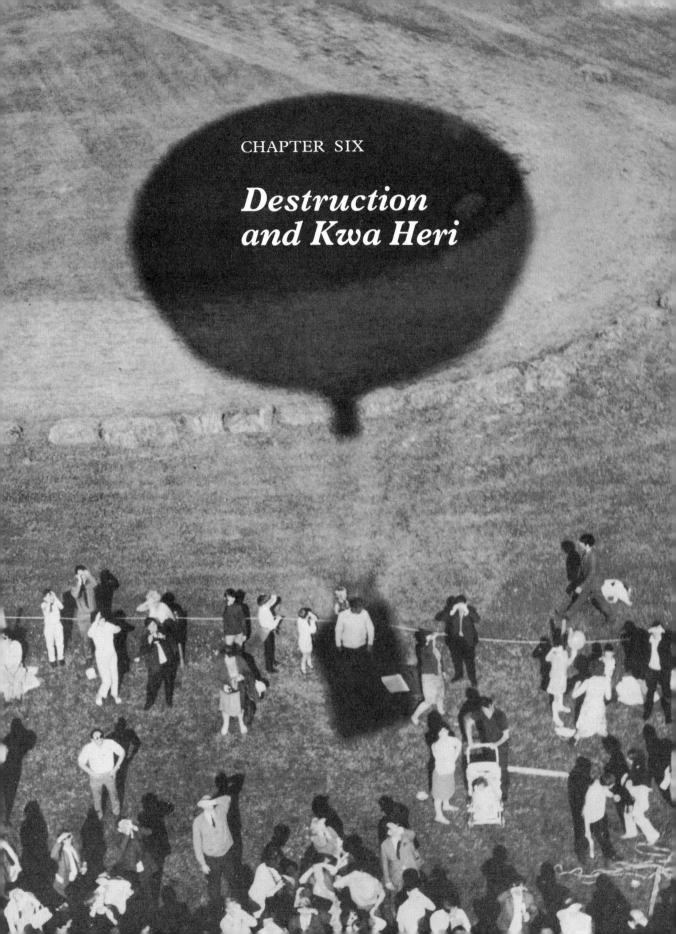

CHAPTER SIX

Destruction and Kwa Heri

The ballooning regulations demand, with good reason, that no one should be in charge of a balloon unless he has had sufficient experience beforehand. Eight flights of a reasonable duration are considered adequate, and the eighth flight has to be made under the supervision of an examiner. One way and another, Malcolm Brighton had spent sufficient time in Jambo, and was ready for his check-out flight. Such flights, are, of course, just as expensive as any other, and he needed a sponsor who would pay for the gas. One was found who warmed most to the idea of a man making his check-out flight by flying across the channel from England to France. Malcolm therefore prepared himself for such a flight. The ideal take-off site, or so he felt, would be Rye in Sussex.

Remarkably the very first aerial crossing of the English Channel had been achieved less than two years after the very first aerial voyage of all time. The trip had been repeated, more or less, on dozens of subsequent attempts, and the lesser occasions had occurred when balloon and crew had fallen short of the target. Even weary and half-deflated balloons have much buoyancy to them, and the various deaths were probably due to cold and exhaustion rather than drowning. An American balloonist had died in 1963 when her balloon had landed in the crowded but cold waters between Catalina Island and the mainland, and Malcolm prepared for his eighth and most testing flight with suitable respect.

At best the journey from Rye needed a wind from the west. To go due east and straight for Cap Gris Nez was most suitable. All other wind directions would lead to longer flights, but Sussex is so well placed with regard to the embracing shape of continental Europe

The last flight took place from Ardingly, Sussex, on a hot summer's day.

that a wind blowing from the north or even from the south of west would also serve to put a balloon on the other side. Rye's own shape is also satisfactory in that the modest bump of land on which this town is built provides good shelter when a westerly wind is blowing. Just below the town, and particularly well protected, is a flat grass field where the sea used to lie during the port's earlier days. On this field and beneath that ancient town Malcolm laid out Jambo and waited for the wind.

It came soon enough and the forecasters at Gatwick promised that the north-westerly airstream would continue. Admittedly it was not my flight, but it was Jambo, and Malcolm had done all his training flights with that balloon. I could not stay away. Down at Rye we all breathed mistily into early morning coffee, and then switched on the gas. It always gave a sense of wonder when this balloon was reborn. The assorted oddities necessary for a balloon flight (see pages twenty-eight-twenty-nine) are so totally unimpressive that it is difficult to see them as the wherewithal for a flying machine. It is hard for most people, but it is hard even for those who have done it all before. The array of objects is more of a disarray, a dismemberment beyond all hope. At that time it is impossible for anyone, balloon operator as much as any other, to imagine a personality belonging to the jumbled assortment lying on the grass. It is ropes. It is canvas and cotton. It is wood and string and a flag. It is parts needing to be transformed into an entity.

With the gas there comes a kind of life. The parts become the whole. Their particular creation becomes the balloon called Jambo, and every time there was this same revitalization. I used to have an animal that slept in a pot. Every once in a while it leapt too energetically from its spherical home, and the whole thing would shatter upon the concrete floor. On each occasion, because it plainly liked its former potted security, I took up all the broken pieces, spread them out, and then started upon the restoration of this other Portland vase. To begin with the animal was entirely disinterested, and let me glue the jagged fragments in peace, but the more the pot grew the more excited the animal became. The final sections of this creature's jig-saw were reinstated because of and despite the general excitement. Within its reformed and well-glued home the animal then slept soundly once again. So too with Jambo. She always became rather more than the sum of her parts.

e flight itself, which ended not too
from Lewes, was uneventful.
mbo was manoeuvred downwind
rer a convenient road, and even
to leap a horse-jump lying
angely in her path.

The fire and the explosion were almost simultaneous. So too were these photographs, the first taken within seconds of the other.

143

The end was quick. The red flame became black smoke and soon there were only fragments. The firemen had need for nothing more than a stirrup pump.

At Rye the man in charge was Malcolm. On board would be Gerry Turnbull, the new official examiner, and every mistake or virtue in the preparation had to be Malcolm's. I helped instead at the gas end, attaching each cylinder in turn, watching them grow frostily cold as they lost their gas, and feeling very distant from the balloon 100 feet away. I did possess a very strong association with that globular thing of orange and silver, of rope and wood. Jambo was a most positive reminder of shared experiences. It had not killed me, and yet I had frequently provided it with plenty of opportunity for doing so. It had not taken me into an African *cu-nim* nor an Alpine peak and had always put me down again, often firmly but surely, on the land where I belonged. So I turned on more and more cylinders of gas and hoped it would do the same for the small party about to leave for the Continent.

Eventually they were ready to go. It was 10.20 a.m. They had thirteen sacks of sand on board and a total of five people. The wind was blowing gently but consistently from the north-west. It stood fair for France. We carried the balloon upwind, and then let them prepare for departure. Quite who all the carriers were on this or on any other occasion, I have no idea. People turn up, and people get given jobs. In fact such people are sized up very quickly and are given tasks according to their obvious capabilities. It is instant recruitment, instant assessment and an equally rapid exploitation. It works very well, and the particular group at Rye stood around to watch them go.

Malcolm weighed off, found equilibrium, poured out a little more sand, and then moved gently downwind. There was a line of poplar trees at the other end of the field and the basket passed effortlessly between two of them. From then on, in traditional fashion, the balloon merely grew smaller and smaller and there was nothing more to report. Instead I felt an aching longing to be with it. What is the point of being on the ground when a balloon, when one's own balloon, is in the air? Like a dockside suddenly bereft of a ship, a take-off field suddenly without its balloon is a place without purpose. The ship and the balloon both grow smaller in their purposefulness and they take their action with them. Moreover I had never seen Jambo take off before: I had always been on board. We all watched that shape disappear to the south-east, and I vowed never again to be left behind. Its dot was all we had to see, but up there they had the whole world beneath them, the muddy sandy world, and then the coast leading west to cliffs and east to the Camber sands. From that moment on they had the Channel beneath them, and Rye itself became a distant dot.

Eventually, round about the time that I was meandering into London via the sclerotic A2, those in the basket had landed successfully at Berck-sur-Mer. The north-westerly wind had disconcertingly changed into a desultory northerly wind, and they had spent time advancing nowhere but digging deep into their sand supplies, before the wind changed back again and took them on to Berck. The people had been welcoming but the customs had been infuriated by this extra cross they had to bear. They impounded the crew, and then the balloon, and they demanded documents and satisfaction. Several hours later they released the crew, and several days later they released the balloon, and that was that save for the

all-important fact that Malcolm successfully achieved SA(L) Form 148 with the mauve diagonal, namely the Board of Trade's Private Pilot's Licence (Balloons and Airships).

Thereafter, armed with this new authority Malcolm and then others became increasingly involved in flying balloons. Suddenly there were ten in the country, and ten pilots to go with them. The balloon club rapidly had plenty of material for its monthly newsletter, and there were 200 club members to receive this regular account of activities. Gerry Turnbull became impressively active, teaching new students and passing out new pilots. The old solitary days had gone for good, but no one could have suspected that the old links were to be severed quite so abruptly.

It was Malcolm who organized that last event. It was as fitting a last event as could have been devised, and was the first of many circumstances which added up to a climax of sentimental introspection. Others might call it mawkish reasoning but I, certainly at the time, and still in quieter moments, feel the disaster to have been most apt, timely, and altogether fitting. That night I would have said that Jambo had caused her self-immolation. Now, over a year after the event, I cannot accept such a ridiculous concept but neither ought I to deny the intensity of this feeling at the time.

It all happened from Ardingly in Sussex. An international balloon event had been arranged as part of a huge summer festival. To one side of the showground, with tents, displays and all the bewildering complexity of a fête bigger than most, the balloons were to be laid out, inflated and launched. Many of the old gang were there: Jo and Nini Boesman, Fred Dolder, François Schaut, Alfred Eckert and Charles Dollfus. I and Jambo were to represent Britain in this international jamboree and we all gathered at a nearby hotel to swap the same old stories. An anticyclone loomed to bless the weekend with its presence.

Down at the field we rolled out Jambo but rather wearily. It had been an active month. Two weeks beforehand the balloon had been flown from Fittleworth in Sussex, as part of the publicity preparations for Ardingly, and had taken six of us pleasantly enough over fields, woods and costly homes up to Godalming in Surrey. A week before it had taken four of us, a somewhat heavier crew, from Newdigate in Surrey on a shorter ride, and we had all landed safely near the turbulence of the Dorking-Reigate road. There were to be flights from Ardingly for all six balloons on both the Saturday and Sunday of that hot weekend.

Saturday's flight was made bizarre by a contrary wind. Toy balloons filled with hydrogen and then released at intervals travelled either due south or due north. In theory we all had to land as close as possible to a point selected by the organizers. Malcolm gave us the choice of two points, one to the north and one to the south, and off we went. Once again there was that feeling of perfection when airborne. Of course trees, streams and fields can be seen from the ground, but they acquire a new dimension from the air. The optimum height is as low as possible, and we brushed along, past treetops, past scurrying pigeons, past the exquisite smells of a summer evening. The wind direction was indeed contrary. With Jambo we went west, but two flew south and the rest flew north. A strange and immortal day.

On the Sunday it was somewhat windier. Again we spread out the balloon, fitted the inflation sleeve and turned on the gas. Again, and for the last time, that splendid shape created itself. Take-off was scheduled for 5 p.m. and all the crews so timed events that they were not prematurely ready. A balloon is most steady when still a firm hemisphere upon the ground. It is least stable, should any wind be blowing, when ready for flight. Jambo was next to a vintage Dutch balloon, first called Oxygenium, then renamed Marco Polo. It had taken me on my first flight and suddenly it and Jambo leant over and bumped each other. Later that night I would have called it an embrace, but in the broad windy daylight both the thought and the action were firmly to be discouraged. We all made haste to go.

My passengers climbed aboard and others had to point out to me various things I was forgetting to do, such as putting the trail rope on board. Later on, following the loss, I was to argue that my obvious carelessness had made me less deserving of such ownership; but, at the time, I merely accepted the trail rope and the rebuff that went with it. One by one the balloons were fired from the ground, as the ground crew let go and the wind took up their charges. Each take-off that day was most rapid, and Jambo was no exception. Very quickly we found ourselves both quite a way downwind and at some 2,000 feet.

On board there were three friends and a television team. These were a girl and a man trying to film and comment upon the peculiar excellence of a balloon flight. The rest of us leant over the edge and watched the trains of the Bluebell line. Before us and behind us were the other aerial corks of the foreign balloons, floating along in a well spaced line. Perhaps it was weariness, perhaps it was foreboding or perhaps the first twinges of boredom, but I felt disenchanted up there. Transporting people from television, and being unexcited by their efforts, was a long way from the reason for which Jambo had been created. Filming the wild-life of Africa seemed exceptionally distant at that moment. Ardingly was not Zanzibar, and that totally wonderful maiden flight to the forests south of Bagamoyo was a world away from the well-tamed map of Sussex-by-the-Sea. I still remembered virtually every fragment of that first flight, almost every word, and was remembering nothing of the talk from Ardingly. Perhaps weariness or perhaps sadness, but I was relieved when we came near the landing zone. I pulled on the valve, and Jambo responded with an even descent to the fields down below.

It was a hayfield in which we actually landed, and we bounced

along as far as we could in order to be near the road. At one time we even bounced over the thorn fence of a horse jump suddenly and unaccountably in our path, but people soon arrived and they carried us over into the next field, one more suitable for deflation. François Schaut was already there, losing the gas from his balloon, and I stopped Jambo upwind of him. Then, having cleared everyone from our immediate area, we too pulled on the valve and heard the gas go out for the last time. It takes a time to go, and we steadily pulled until the fabric itself began to fall to the ground. I left the basket, and then a gust blew big spinnaker shapes into the balloon. I tried to rip to lose all the gas, and had pulled briefly on the rope when there was a sudden rush of sound. It was a noisy whoosh at first and then it was a bang. The balloon had caught fire and had then exploded.

Very quickly the burning fabric fell to the ground. I saw my hands were unburnt and walked around the fire terrified that someone might have walked under the balloon at the very last moment. I kicked all accessible burning bits, but they didn't feel like burning limbs. Not for five minutes, or was it ten or one, was I able to walk through the middle and find no one. The borrowed basket was unharmed. The borrowed ring, a thing of wood and rope and nearer the fire, was equally untouched. I too, standing nearest of all, was not even singed. Only Jambo, the net and that orange and silver fabric, had gone and it had gone entirely. There was black grass, and soon there were firemen and police but there was nothing much for them to see.

The recovery team were there and they helped to put the basket, the ring and other various oddments into the van. There was nothing for the large canvas sacks, and we threw them into the basket with a sad effortlessness. When full those sacks had caused countless Africans, and Alpini, and Belgians and Dutch, and innumerable Englishmen who appeared in so many fields to grunt and laugh and express amazement at the weight. Now those sacks were empty, and we also emptied the remaining sacks of sand into a heap on that blackened grass. *Jambo* means Hello in Swahili, and we had given her that name when over the Straits of Zanzibar. *Kwa heri* means goodbye and I patted down that pile of sand before scratching these two other Swahili words on to its surface with a piece of twig. I also put the date.

And that, as they say, was that, although no one said much as we left that final field. It is unthinkable that one should credit fabric and rope with a personality. It is unpardonable to imagine it capable of self-destruction. It is ridiculous even to wonder at such a destruction, or to be amazed that it could be achieved with so little damage to anything else. That evening, with the smell of the fire still on our hands and clothes and when on the way back to a chastened hotel, I suspect that each of us imagined and thought about all these things. A balloon, any balloon, does have a touch of magic about it; and Jambo had been more remarkable than most. Someone even said as we left that field: 'I don't suppose things will ever be quite the same again.' Probably not. A piece of oneself had gone for good.

ACKNOWLEDGEMENTS

A remarkable feature of this book is the co-operation that it received during its creation. The idea of writing it, and of displaying as many relevant photographs as possible, arose shortly after Jambo's fiery end. It became quickly apparent, when people wrote expressing sympathy, that a tremendous store of photographs existed. That final landing, for example, had been recorded seemingly from every angle and most effectively before and after the holocaust. If there were so many pictures of this one occasion it was probable, or so we argued, that there must be thousands more depicting all the other occasions on which Jambo flew. Therefore the task was to try and collect them.

The energy for this formidable endeavour was supplied by Jill Southam. She wrote hundreds of letters. She followed up every lead she was given. She wrote to friends of friends who thought other friends might have taken a picture. Local newspapers gave her letters wider publicity, and soon the photographs were pouring in. All in all about 3,000 were received and they were each accompanied by considerable support for the idea of this book. Therefore, to Jill Southam in particular, and to all those others who responded to her request, Douglas Botting and myself are enormously grateful. We hope we have done justice to all this enthusiasm.

The long list below gives the names of those who helped. Not all their photographs could be chosen, but we are grateful to all for the trouble they took in responding to our call. Without them this book would not have been possible. (After the names of those whose photographs *have* been chosen are the numbers of the pages on which their photographs appear, together with copyright details in instances where the photographer does not own the copyright.) To these people and organisations we are, of course, additionally grateful.

Henry Adlam; Air Products; G. E. Andrews (facing 113 top left); D Archer, Gloucestershire Gazette; Artistes Associés (102, 103); Associated Newspapers (18 top right); James Astor (90, 91, 94, 95); Michael Astor; Austrian National Tourist Office; Barnaby's Picture Library; Roger Barrett; Martyn Beckett (25 top, 109 bottom, 119 left); Lewis Benjamin; Graham Berry; R. W. Bird and J. A. Wright, East of England Show; Birmingham Post and Mail; Richard Bladon; John Blake; Eric Buston & Associates.

Jo Boesman; Kenneth Bolton, East African Standard; Douglas Botting (16, 21, 22–3, 25 bottom, 28–9, 30, 31, facing 33, 34, 36, 37, 38–9, 40, 42, 43, 44, 45, 46 top, 47, facing 49, 50, 51, 60, 61, 66–67, 74, 79 bottom right, 80 bottom left, 93, facing 96, 112, facing 112, 116, 118 centre and bottom left, 125 centre, facing 129, 130, 132, 133, facing 145, 150, 152); Leslie W. Botting; Thomas Bourhill; Brian Branston; Malcolm Brighton (104 left, 109 top); British Broadcasting Corporation; Russell Brockbank (80 top – courtesy of Punch); Maurice Broomfield (53); Charles E. Brown (15 top); Ronald Brownlow.

Butch Calderwood (56 right, 76); Giles Camplin; J. Allan Cash; Martin Child; Clayton Studios (82, 122 left and centre – courtesy of Port Sunlight Magazine); Comet Photo AG (14, 78); John Cope; Mrs. John Cura; Daily Telegraph (86 top); Peter Davey (88–9); S. B. Davie; R. Dawson; Wilhelm Debus (58); Fred Dolder; Charles Dollfus; Alfred Eckert (facing 48, 76–7, facing 97, facing 114 bottom); F. Engesser (63, 64–5, 75 – copyright Swiss Tourist Office, Zurich); Robert English.

Janet Ferguson; Field & Crane (109 centre); Beryl Fogg (138); Philippe Gaussot (102 top); James Gilbert; J. R. Gilbert; Chris Gittins; John Goode;

ACKNOWLEDGEMENTS

Robin Goodman; Jennifer Greaves; Barry Griffiths; The Grower; Guy Hallart (136 top); John Hanson; Wilfred Harper; David Harris; Neil Harrison; Anthony Heaney; Dieter Heggemann (71, 72–3, 79 bottom left – copyright Der Stern); Elizabeth Hewison; John Higgins (98); David Hillier (facing 32); Tony Holland, who redrew his cartoon for the book (107 – courtesy New Scientist); Gordon Hughesdon (facing 113 bottom right, 137, 141 left); I. R. Hunt; Vic Hunter; Gerald Isaaman, Hampstead & Highgate Express; Italian State Tourist Office; Richard Jahre; Jean Jules-Verne; J. E. Kelly, Oxo Ltd; E. G. Lambert (88 centre); Hugh Lamprey (48); Lance Studios.

Max Lenz (69 top); Jean Lesqui; Anne Lewis-Smith; Monty Lister (119 right); Gerry Long; Ruth Macdonald; H. McKinstrie; Bill Malpas; Martin (146–7 – copyright Sunday Express); David Monk; Pierre Monnier (centre spread between 56 and 57 top right); Martin Mücke (85); Colin Mudie; Gordon Murray; Mürren Tourist Office (55); Gillian Nassau; Harry Nelson; Beryl Noble; Flavia Nunes; Observer/Camera Press (109 right, 124 left, 126, facing 128, facing 129 top, 135 bottom); R. W. Pearce.

John Pickett, Horatio Myer & Co; Stanley Pittman, City of Birmingham Parks Department; Paul Popper Ltd; Press Association (86 bottom); Michael Price (18 bottom right, 105, 110, 118 top and bottom right, 119 bottom); Michael Rayward, Shrewsbury Information Bureau; Francis Redfern; David Richardson (122 right); Bill Roberts, British American Tobacco Co; John Robson, Greater Nottingham Co-operative Society; Michael Rolfe (facing 144 top); Alan Root (40, 62 bottom); Joan Root (32); Crispin Rose-Innes; P. M. Rowlatt; Royal Aeronautical Society.

Peter Sadler; Tom Sage (19, 27 bottom, 56 left, facing 56 top and bottom, facing 57, 79 top left, facing 113 top right and bottom left, 114, 117, 120, 124 bottom right, 124–5, 125 right, 131); Erwin Sautter (centre spread between 56 and 57 top left and bottom right, 59, 62 top, 69); François Schaut; D. W. Selmes; Edwin Shackleton; Marion Sherman, Horniblow, Cox-Freeman Intnl; The Rev. D. A. P. Shields; Albert Sijthoff; Susan Smith; Albert Spencer; Swiss National Tourist Office, London; Syndication International (15 bottom, 121, 128, 134, 135 top, 136 bottom); J. E. Tate; Alan Taylor (88 bottom); Leonard Taylor; Barry Tempest; Mrs. J. B. Thirlwell; Gresham Thompson.

The Times (127); Topix (18 bottom left, 52, 88 top, 125 left, 139); Gerry Turnbull; Twentieth Century Fox (104 right); United Artists (100 – from The Bed Sitting Room directed by Richard Lester); Jean-Pierre van den Bemden (27 top); Lord Ventry; Jules Verne (13, 149 – from Five Weeks in a Balloon); Tom Wadden; James Millar Watt (17); J. H. A. K. Gualthérie van Weezel; William Wheeler; F. White, The People; David Wilson; Wiltshire Newspapers (81, 83, 96); Max Woosnam; David Yeandel; A. J. Young (141 right, 142, 143, 144); P. Zaugg, Photoglob – Wehrli A. G. (centre spread between 56 and 57 bottom left).

PASSENGERS

To fly in the enforced confines of a balloon's basket is to join a special kind of club. Here, for the record, is as complete a passenger list as we could contrive of all those who flew in Jambo.

Anthony Smith
Douglas Botting
Charl Pauw
Alan Root
John Newbould
Geoffrey Hancock
Anthony Meeren
Nini Boesman
J. H. A. K. Gualthérie van
                    Weezel
Albert Sijthoff
Albert van den Bemden
Josef Vanderstraeten
Jean-Marie Dubreucq
Charles Dollfus
Norman Williams
Mary West
Peter Kevan
George Ross
Max Woosnam
Niall Henessy
Graham Tidman
Malcolm Brighton
Joy Hill
Paula Veliz
Jo Boesman
Michael Price
Roger Barrett

Tim Matthews
Charles Meisl
Jacqueline Sax
Albert Finney
Peter Sushitsky
Giles Camplin
Roger Myer
Gerry Turnbull
Christine Turnbull
Doddy Hay
Jenny Hay
Kees Jansen
Karen Kersten
Paul Pickering
Graham Berry
John Dalling
Don Cameron
David Yeandel
Barry Wallace
Mike Rolfe
Jean Herbé
John Bond
Wilfred Harper
Crispin Rose-Innes
Alyth Ball
Monty Lister
Christopher Lock
Tim Godfrey

Amanda Jones
Kate Pollard
Ted Hull
Michael Astor
Alan McGlashan
James Astor
Pinky Beckett
Marina Warner
Claire Ridley
Thomas McGinn
Ann Clark
Gordon Clark
Spray Mallaby
Joanna Rose-Innes
Flavia Nunes
William Wheeler
Peter Hall
Anne Lewis-Smith
Mark Westwood
Jean Lesqui
Hazel Earle
Joyce Rhodes
Mike Kennedy
Dianne Rigby
Jill Southam
Christine Rolfe
David Harris
Gordon Hughesdon

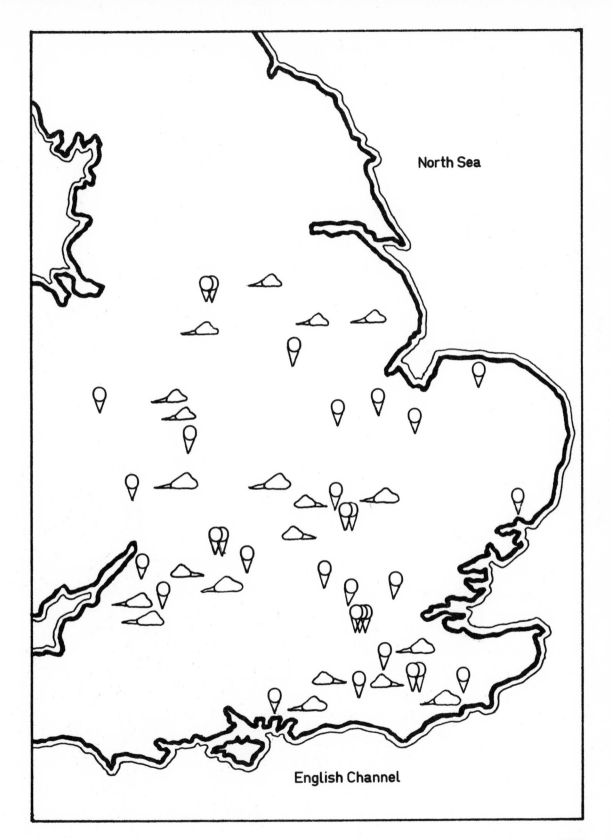

North Sea

English Channel

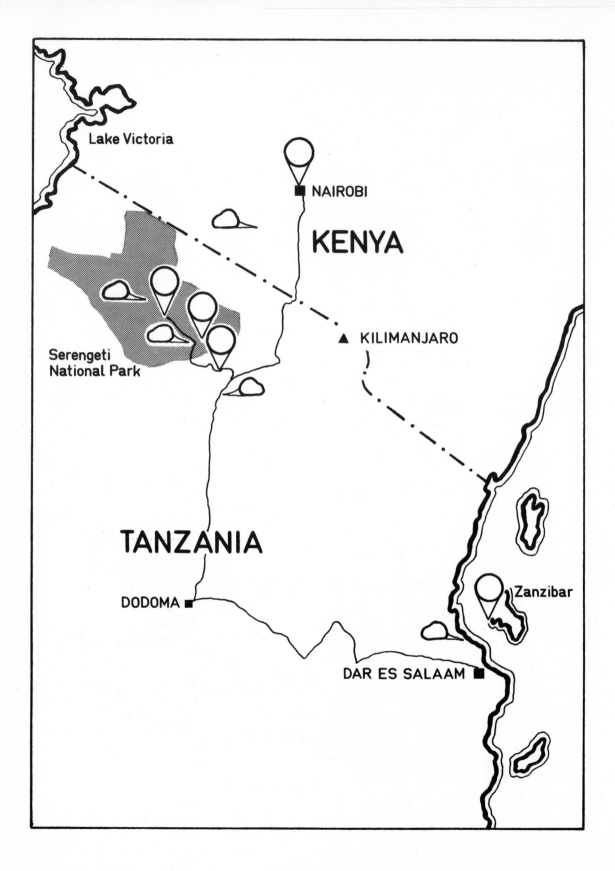